D0769919

"Fourteen years after the events of their succe[ss] *[Parallel] Worlds*, Gottlieb and Graham headed back to Co[te] to conduct research and share the proceeds of th[eir] monizing narratives, *Braided Worlds* recounts this return to Bengland, offering a tale filled with intelligence, humor, and humility. Gottlieb and Graham invite readers to travel with grace and insight through the external landscape of Africa and the internal geography of marriage, parenthood, and ethical living. I would accompany them anywhere." —Michele Morano, author of *Grammar Lessons: Translating a Life in Spain*

"More than a sequel to the much-celebrated *Parallel Worlds*—which entranced several generations of my students—*Braided Worlds* takes readers deep into the heart of West Africa today, treating the fraught encounters and ethical dilemmas of anthropological fieldwork with remarkable empathy. A beautiful book that resists romance while remaining soulful, *Braided Worlds* is filled with seductive storytelling and sparkling prose." —Charlie Piot, author of *Remotely Global: Village Modernity in West Africa*

"In this lively, engaging memoir, Gottlieb and Graham conjure the confluence of multiple experiences and worlds. Their deep connection with the Beng people over the years offers an authoritative and, even more important, a touchingly personal account of life in one West African culture. This book is a wonderful addition to our contemporary creative nonfiction literature, combining the best of immersion journalism, personal memoir, and academic study into a delightful and enchanting narrative. This literary journey reminds us, again and again, of the unbreakable bonds of our common humanity." —Xu Xi, author of *Habit of a Foreign Sky: A Novel*

"*Braided Worlds* is a gripping and instructive curl-up-in-a-chair book, appealing to anthropologists, Africanists, and to travelers and wannabe travelers who like to think and read across cultures and about fascinating encounters. The memoir weaves together the alternating voices of an anthropologist and a writer, both keen observers of character and context, and unforgettable local actors such as Alma's friend Amenan, the mad-to-be-modern Matatu, and the authors' young son, Nathaniel, with his Beng buddies. Through moving stories, such as that of Philip's father's African afterlife, we get a sense of worlds once parallel that have become progressively braided over time. Having successfully taught *Parallel Worlds*, I like *Braided Worlds* even more, and plan to use it in courses on fieldwork ethics, anthropological writing, and African ethnography." —Pamela Feldman-Savelsberg, Carleton College

PRAISE FOR *PARALLEL WORLDS*

"A beautiful memoir that will be savored with pleasure by seasoned fieldworkers, about-to-be fieldworkers, and anyone who is simply a fieldworker of the imagination." —Sherry Ortner, author of *New Jersey Dreaming: Capital, Culture, and the Class of '58*

A remarkable look at a remote society [and] an engaging memoir that testifies to a loving partnership. . . . Compelling." —James Idema, *Chicago Tribune*

"A marvelously detailed and intriguing account of the hazards attending an attempt to embrace a radically different culture. . . . A unique collaborative achievement." —Norman Rush, author of *Mating*

"*Parallel Worlds* is that miraculous nonfiction book which reads so compellingly that one goes to bed wondering what will happen next and wakes up glad to find that there are still pages to go. It merges our own parallel lives as professionals who seek out ethnographies from duty and as readers who surrender to an engrossing book with joy." —Kirin Narayan, *Anthropology and Humanism*

"Powerful. . . . [The authors] lead the reader on an adventurous journey. . . . Offers Western readers a broader view of the state of affairs in Ivory Coast and of the continent's vast complexities." —Mwangi Ireri, *Christian Science Monitor*

"An intelligent, adventurous young married couple, Gottlieb and Graham arrived in Bengland with open minds, both eager for Gottlieb to begin her first serious fieldwork as a 'novice anthropologist.' Their beautifully written accounts of living with the Beng serve as a vivid testament to the fact that people of different cultures can find common ground." —Ann Collette, *Creative Nonfiction*

"As their lives converge and ultimately meld with those of the Beng people in common humanity—childbirth, celebration, sickness and death—this book becomes strangely affirming of homo sapiens. In alternating passages, Ms. Gottlieb and Mr. Graham plot that convergence in precise, often arresting prose." —Marvin Hunt, the *Atlanta Journal-Constitution*

"This volume breaks new ground by its artful integration of two writers' voices, offering a remarkable and engaging expression of parallel worlds." —George Marcus, coeditor of *Writing Culture*

"A book of unusual candor, *Parallel Worlds* offers a unique introduction to Africa." —H. James Birx, *Library Journal*

BRAIDED WORLDS

Alma Gottlieb & Philip Graham

THE UNIVERSITY OF CHICAGO PRESS

Chicago and London

Alma Gottlieb is professor of anthropology at the University of Illinois at Urbana-Champaign. She is the author of *The Restless Anthropologist, The Afterlife Is Where We Come From,* and *Under the Kapok Tree,* all published by the University of Chicago Press. **Philip Graham** is professor of creative writing at the University of Illinois at Urbana-Champaign, and also teaches at the Vermont College of Fine Arts. He is the author of seven books of fiction and nonfiction, including *The Moon, Come to Earth,* also published by the University of Chicago Press. Together they are the authors of *Parallel Worlds: An Anthropologist and a Writer Encounter Africa.*

The University of Chicago Press, Chicago 60637
The University of Chicago Press, Ltd., London
© 2012 by Alma Gottlieb and Philip Graham
All rights reserved. Published 2012.
Printed in the United States of America

21 20 19 18 17 16 15 14 13 12   1 2 3 4 5

ISBN-13: 978-0-226-30527-1 (cloth)
ISBN-13: 978-0-226-30528-8 (paper)
ISBN-13: 978-0-226-30472-4 (e-book)
ISBN-10: 0-226-30527-9 (cloth)
ISBN-10: 0-226-30528-7 (paper)
ISBN-10: 0-226-30472-8 (e-book)

Library of Congress Cataloging-in-Publication Data

Gottlieb, Alma
    Braided worlds / Alma Gottlieb and Philip Graham.
        pages. cm.
    Includes index.
    ISBN-13: 978-0-226-30527-1 (cloth: alkaline paper)
    ISBN-10: 0-226-30527-9 (cloth: alkaline paper)
    ISBN-13: 978-0-226-30528-8 (paperback: alkaline paper)
    ISBN-10: 0-226-30528-7 (paperback: alkaline paper)
    [etc.]
    1. Beng (African people)—Social life and customs.   2. Philosophy, Beng.   3. Beng (African people)—Religion.   4. Ethnology—Fieldwork—Côte d'Ivoire.   5. Côte d'Ivoire—Social life and customs.   6. Côte d'Ivoire—Description and travel.   I. Graham, Philip, 1951–   II. Title.
    DT545.45.B45G72 2012
    305.896'34—dc23
                                    2011050823

♾ This paper meets the requirements of ANSI/NISO Z39.48-1992 (Permanence of Paper).

For the Beng people,

and for Nathaniel

Contents

Photos, reading guides, and other supporting materials for this book can be found at: http://www.press.uchicago.edu/sites/braidedworlds/.

Preface

The Beng people of Côte d'Ivoire have challenged, enlightened, haunted, and inspired us for most of our adult lives.

In 1979–80, during our first, fifteen-month stay in the tiny village of Kosangbé in one corner of the West African rain forest, Alma conducted research for her doctorate in anthropology, while Philip worked on his first short-story collection—stories that were increasingly influenced by the experience of living in a radically different culture. In 1985, we returned to Bengland to live in the larger village of Asagbé; Alma continued the research that would lead to her first full-length ethnography of the Beng, and Philip began working on the fictions that eventually became his second story collection. Yet no matter how deeply we delved into the worldviews of the Beng people of Côte d'Ivoire, and how close some of our friendships grew, we reluctantly conceded that our lives would likely remain forever separated by unbridgeable cultural gulfs—parallel lines, never quite converging. Hence the title for the memoir we published (in 1993) about the stories that enveloped us during our first two visits: *Parallel Worlds*.

In 1993, we lived in Bengland for a third time, and this last stay serves as the main focus of *Braided Worlds*. Here we recount a different cultural encounter from that of our first memoir. The multileveled cultural world of the Beng ultimately had come to inhabit us both, suggesting a potential connection far more intimate than parallel lines, and shaping much of our lives outside of Africa—including how we approached the most intimate decisions we made concerning the birth and parenting of our first child. During our third trip to Bengland—this time, with our six-year-old son—our lives intertwined so much with those of our Beng friends and adoptive families that, finally, they became inextricably braided. This companion memoir chronicles the surprising turns and challenges of that unfolding process.

Braided Worlds, like *Parallel Worlds* before it, presents our encounters with what most Westerners would consider an "other" culture by interweaving stories of both villagers and visitors. In so doing, the double perspectives of a writer's eye and an anthropologist's concerns emerge through narrative. (We present our equal writing partnership only via the accident of alphabetic placement.) Thus this memoir is sung in a different key from that of conventional scholarly discussions of life in rural Africa. For one thing, even in this age of reflexive looks at what and how we write, many anthropologists work hard to produce cultural and political analyses that are so persuasive that the person behind the analysis remains invisible. One aim of both our previous memoir and this companion volume, then, is to pull back the curtain during rehearsal, allowing readers to witness the personal struggles and transformations that precede and accompany cultural understanding.

At the same time, our memoir is a literary construction of deep travel, the culmination of fourteen years of cultural encounter. Too often, even the best-intentioned travel memoirs skim the surface, offering well-crafted observations limited by mere weeks or months of experience abroad. Years of engagement, however, reveal—like an unfolding Mandelbrot set—ever finer scales of complexity, multiple layers of truth that often humble a traveler's early assumptions.

The events of the pages that follow begin in the United States in the fall of 1986, just a year after we had returned from Alma's second period of field research in Bengland. Following an account of Philip's short trip to Côte d'Ivoire for a writers' conference in 1990, which chronicles that country's first serious outbreak of political turmoil, the bulk of *Braided Worlds* recounts our return to Bengland in 1993. Our book comes full circle in 1994, when we recount the culture shock that marked a young Beng man's arrival in America. Throughout the arc of these accumulating narratives, we also trace the downward political and economic spiral that eventually plunged the West African nation into sporadic civil war, and our memoir trains a microscopic lens on the national challenges typically discussed at a more macro level, illustrating their effects—depression, despair, even madness—on ordinary and powerless villagers. Serious issues surrounding Africa saturate both this and our previous memoir—critiques of power inequities, racialized histories, colonial legacies, and discourses of othering—but at implicit rather than explicit levels, through the juxtapositions and unexpected convergences of stories that constitute the narrative argument of the book.

Though written in the past tense, *Braided Worlds* aims to re-create the immediacy of the present-moment external drama of our lives among the Beng people, as well as the drama of our internal states. In adopting this literary nonfiction writing strategy, which resists after-the-fact explanations and moralizing intrusions from our future selves, we reconstruct both our day-to-day foibles and failures, and our genuine wonder—for, as we have discovered even after three extended stays among the Beng, the quest for cultural understanding deepens and complicates in such a way that surprises are always possible.

Finally, in writing *Braided Worlds*, we have been careful to confirm the accuracy of the events we narrate here by relying on Alma's extended field notes and taped interviews, Philip's writing notebooks, and the numerous photos and videos we took during the summer of 1993, all of which collectively provided detailed information about virtually every day of our stay. Still, on some occasions, we have had to rely on our memories of events—what some anthropologists call "head notes"—particularly in reconstructing the details of conversations. Nathaniel Gottlieb-Graham and Bertin Kouadio have shared their own recollections of events in which they participated. Ultimately, though, the accuracy of the stories that follow rests on our shoulders. Through the braiding of first-person narratives, we portray the ongoing conversation that our American family has had over the years with our Beng family: attempting to engage with another way of being, to learn from another set of postulates, to chip away at the seductive assumption that the world can be explained by a single narrative.

A Note to Readers

This book starts in the middle.

Following the time-honored techniques of nonfiction memoir writing, we open our narrative in midstream, taking our readers on a journey whose history predates these pages and whose future awaits. For those who prefer more background before traversing an unfamiliar landscape, we refer you to the final pages of this memoir, where "A Brief Note about the Beng" can provide a preview of the people you will encounter here. The epilogue updates the reader on the course of Côte d'Ivoire's civil war, its impact on the Beng community, and the contemporary situation of the Beng as of this writing. To keep track of the names of the people who populate this memoir, the reader may wish to consult the "Cast of Characters," while a glossary provides help with French and Beng terms. Our memoir's end pages also feature four maps: one situates Bengland within a larger map of Côte d'Ivoire; a second map highlights the villages and roads of the Beng area; a third map gives a more intimate look at a single Beng compound; and a fourth map places the Beng region in the context of the civil war.

For those interested in a fuller discussion of the research that Alma conducted on Beng infant care in summer 1993, we refer readers to her full-length study, *The Afterlife Is Where We Come From: The Culture of Infancy in West Africa* (University of Chicago Press, 2004). For those curious about the novel that Philip was completing while living in Asagbé, we refer them to *How to Read an Unwritten Language* (Scribner, 1995; Warner Books, 1997).

A Beng Path to Birth

SEPTEMBER 1986 – MAY 1987

ALMA: OF BLESSINGS AND BAD FAITH

A young girl pestered her grandmother's purse for hidden candy while beside them a toddler nuzzled into his mother's lap, and in the corner a weary-eyed mother nursed an eager infant as twin boys chased each other in circles. Though sitting in an obstetrician's office in the Midwest, surrounded by children I felt transported back to West Africa, where kids far outnumber grown-ups.

Whenever I'd given a Beng village neighbor the gift of a smoked fish, an aspirin, or an orange, she usually thanked me with, "May god give you many, many, many children!" I'd felt guilty every time I accepted one of these blessings, but I always held my tongue. Philip and I had lived childless in Africa, and I knew these friends from another culture would find our use of contraceptives incomprehensible. Why would a young couple delay pregnancy? Now, just a year after our second extended stay among the Beng, I still heard those voices, could still vividly remember sitting beside my friend Amenan in the dusty courtyard of her family's compound, while an ever-changing group of children played among young women who pounded long pestles into huge wooden mortars to prepare the next meal.

The nurse called the woman with twins across from me, and as the two boys tagged along behind their mother, I squeezed Philip's hand. Last week we participated in the modern bathroom ritual of watching an e.p.t dipstick turn from white to blue, a seemingly magical transformation that would surely impress my Beng women friends.

Then our turn came to leave the waiting room. Inside my doctor's office, the framed diplomas from impressive universities called to me as a diviner's reputation called to my Beng friends. Even if the doctor merely corroborated what my body already knew, I craved the authority of his pronouncement.

To our surprise, my Father Knows Best–looking doctor started off by asking, "Have you done an e.p.t test?"

"Actually, yes," I answered, "and it came out positive."

"Well, then, you're pregnant. Those home tests are quite accurate, so let's calculate when this baby will come out." He plotted out numbers on his calendar. "Looks like the first of May to me."

The date made our news feel real—even if I knew few women who gave birth on their due dates. We each have our belief systems, I reminded myself, and mine comes in white coats. Or maybe my Beng neighbors' blessings had worked their magic at last—despite my having accepted them at the time in bad faith.

After Philip and I thanked the doctor and scheduled a follow-up appointment, we linked arms and headed for the parking lot.

"Who do we call first?" Philip gushed with his usual enthusiasm.

"Hmmm," I replied, more cautious. "Our folks, for sure . . ."

I needed time to sort out my thoughts. As Philip unlocked the car doors, I pictured a Beng woman weeding fields while her baby slept on the ground nearby, guarded by a dog; or picking coffee beans, an infant tied to her back; or washing laundry aided by her two-year-old daughter splashing water happily on the clothes. In Beng villages, parents *expect* to work while surrounded by children. In Illinois, I taught in classrooms with hard linoleum floors and bright fluorescent lights—no soft soil underfoot, no sunlight filtering through an overhanging canopy of leaves. I rarely heard my university colleagues talk about their families, rarely saw their children at work, and there was no private lounge in which I might comfortably nurse my infant. The famous "juggling work and motherhood" mantra that so many women journalists invoked in their feature stories suddenly felt scarily close. I'd need to figure out how to negotiate my own juggling act in the academic slice of the middle class where I lived my life.

≋ In the aisles of the maternity section, I walked past a row of pink T-shirts proclaiming "Baby inside" and eyed racks of wide elastic waistbands and ungainly panels set into huge polyester pants. Now in my seventh week, another part of Africa asserted itself: the urge to relish rather than conceal my impending motherhood. But paying high prices for ugly clothes to announce my new state seemed unfair. In a Beng village, I would simply tie my long wraparound skirt a bit more loosely each week, and—presto—my maternity wardrobe would be complete.

Finally I found an innocuous blue-and-white-striped shirt and navy skirt that I wouldn't feel embarrassed to wear. True, the pleated blouse puffed out more than my still slightest hint of bulge. Though I now felt ready to announce my growing body, I dreaded the phrase "You're showing," which didn't sound friendly. In American women's lives, what "shows" usually isn't meant to: bra straps, panty lines, slip hems. If my pregnancy were "showing," was I supposed to somehow tuck it in like underwear?

≋ I squirted some honey into my cup of chamomile tea, feeling smug that I'd sworn off chocolate, black tea, and wine a month before becoming pregnant. Maybe I'm having such an easy time because I'm so careful about my diet, I boasted silently. No morning sickness, no lower back pain, not even weird midnight food cravings. If anything, I felt more energetic than usual. But whenever I revealed my good luck to any friend who'd already given birth, I discovered in the awkward silence that the discourse of pregnancy in America is often a discourse of punishment: Eve all over again.

My food restrictions were nothing like those my Beng friend Amenan observed while pregnant. She always passed up bushbuck meat so her baby's skin wouldn't come out patchy like the striped coat of that small antelope; and while walking through the forest to her fields, she never brought along leftovers from a meal. If she carelessly dropped some morsels on the path, any nearby snake might eat them, and that would spell disaster: finding the food delicious, the serpent would long for more tasty tidbits and its spirit would enter the human fetus . . . dooming the expectant mother to deliver a snake, in the form of a severely disabled child. I flinched at the thought. These days, I didn't need to believe in snake children to tap into every pregnant woman's elemental fear of a baby born with disabilities.

Sipping from my warm cup, I paged through a book from the pile of parenting manuals Philip and I had accumulated. Raised as an only child, I felt hopelessly under-prepared for the practicalities of parenting. Nor did these books reassure me, with their endless lists of warnings: Don't let your baby sleep too long, or eat too much, or go more than a day without a bath, otherwise this, otherwise that. Before your baby starts to crawl, one book advised, you'd better get down on hands and knees and look up, imagining the room from an infant's perspective. Then you could anticipate a yanked cord that might topple a floor lamp onto your young crawler, or notice an electric wall outlet that might invite curious fingers. Horrors abounded . . . yet they paled before the risks of stepping on a scorpion, drinking water harboring dangerous parasites, or being bitten by malarial mosquitoes—all perils facing Beng children I'd known.

≋ "N no n seyenlo," I whispered to myself.

The Beng phrase usually meant, "I have a stomach-ache." But lying on my side, I embodied its other meaning. One day soon after I'd arrived in the village of Asagbé, my friend Amenan's mother had seen me in the market.

"Amenan has a stomach-ache," the elderly woman told me.

Missing the nuances of the phrase I thought I knew, I'd bought some more tomatoes and onions before proceeding to Amenan's house—where I saw my friend lying on her side in labor, and suddenly understood that "stomach-ache" could double for "having contractions."

Now I squirmed to find comfort on our bed, which couldn't quite cushion the hours of pain that seemed to stretch before me with no end in sight. Right after my waters broke, I'd glanced in the mirror and thought: After tomorrow, my image will forever be that of a mother. But when I heard Philip opening and closing drawers, preparing a suitcase for the hospital, I said, "Not yet. I wonder how far along I am, though."

Hewing to the logic of science—when things get rough, we measure— Philip timed my contractions and dutifully recorded them in a notebook. But in many ways I feared this logic, well aware of research chronicling the need-less risks that high-tech births can bring to low-risk pregnancies. Too many American women reported feeling MIA at their own deliveries. The less time in a white-walled room filled with IV drips and beeping monitors, the less chance I'd end up with an unnecessary episiotomy or cesarean.

The Beng way of birth relies on the laboring woman's body, rather than ma-chines, as the most important source of information. Though I yearned for the extended community of Beng women, I wasn't so naïve as to ignore the risks of birthing at home. Knowing laboring Beng women who'd suffered greatly— and even some who'd died—prevented me from romanticizing a home deliv-ery. Throughout my pregnancy, I'd felt caught between the competing visions of a hospital birth and a home birth. Philip and I agonized over where and how to have this baby until Laura offered her services.

Finishing medical school at the same time that she was writing a master's thesis in anthropology about American midwives, Laura proved a perfect coach. Together, we devised a compromise strategy: once my labor started, I'd stay home as long as possible, leaving for the hospital at the last possible min-ute. A late arrival to the maternity ward could keep my labor progressing and my mood calm without subjecting me to the Pitocin drips and anesthesia that would drug me and my unborn child.

"Do you think it's too late to call Laura?" I asked Philip.

"She said to call whenever your waters broke," he said, so I did.

After sleepily grilling me on the timing of my contractions, Laura pronounced that I was still in early labor, then graciously offered to spend the rest of the night in our guest room. Philip and Laura alternated a few hours of sleep; I was too pained—and excited—to do anything but lie wide-eyed in our dark bedroom, trying to recall the name of the plant that Beng women use to hasten a delivery, massaging my belly spasms, and changing positions every few minutes to settle into the quickening contractions.

At the first light of dawn, I roused Philip. He massaged my back and shoulders, but his kneading hands could do nothing to soften the contractions.

"N no n seyenlo, n no n seyenlo," I repeated to myself in Beng—I have a stomach-ache, I have a stomach-ache.

PHILIP: THE SCRABBLE CHAMPION

Shortly after Laura woke and took her turn tending to Alma, I felt the urge to calm my nerves, if only for a few minutes. A handful of unpaid bills and a story manuscript for my agent offered a plausible excuse to head off to the neighborhood mailbox.

"How far is it?" Laura asked.

"Not very far," I replied, a touch defensive that Laura might think I was deserting my post—after all, I could more easily leave my handful of envelopes out for the mail carrier in the front-door chute. "Maybe three blocks."

She turned to Alma. "Why don't you go along? You know, walking helps move the baby down the birth canal."

Alma and I exchanged skeptical looks, but Laura added, "Don't worry, at this rate of Alma's contractions, we still have a few hours to go."

After a little more encouragement, Alma and I headed outside. A lone car idled by, then left the road to its usual morning quiet. A glorious blue sky and warm spring breeze greeted us as we walked down the steps to the sidewalk. Trees and banks of flowers bloomed everywhere, the entire world offering us an example of growth and new life. Now those three blocks seemed stretched out to something more like three hundred miles. Though Alma and I had embraced certain aspects of a Beng style of birth, I couldn't imagine any village couple embarking on a jaunt like this.

We proceeded slowly, arms linked, stopping whenever Alma felt another surge of pain wash over her; a few times she stopped to lean against a tree. I couldn't shake the distressing thought of her delivering our baby on the sidewalk, as the distant blue mailbox seemed a mirage, receding ever farther. Through our slow progress, time seemed suspended, linking us in a way we'd never felt linked before, encased in a bubble all our own, and soon enough we didn't care where the hell that mailbox was.

Eventually I slipped the various envelopes in the slot, with the sobering thought that this was the last mail I'd post before becoming a father. Then we turned and began the walk back home. A backpack-laden student striding to campus caught sight of us and stared—unsettled, perhaps, by the strange spectacle of a woman obviously in labor taking a morning stroll with her husband through a suburban neighborhood.

≋   Thirty-seven more points. As Alma tallied up her score so far, I scanned the Scrabble board for any decent purchase, any small corner where I might eke out a reasonable number of points from my lousy collection of letters—a maddening batch of vowelsvowelsvowels, though of course I lacked a u for my lone consonant, q.

I lagged hopelessly behind. Laura managed a little better, but we both trailed in the distant dust of Alma's impressive score. Alma picked five new tiles from the bag, pausing a few long seconds as a new contraction stiffened her face. I held her free hand, accepted the crush of her fingers.

Alma's labor had edged into its twelfth hour. Who knew how much longer we'd have to wait before our child was born? *Dilate, dilate,* I silently prayed, while my eyes searched the board for anywhere I might attach a couple of vowels and make a creditable little word.

"Let's check you again," Laura said, once the contraction faded, and she and Alma left our back porch for the living room.

At six centimeters, we'd haul off to the hospital. Although part of me wanted that time to arrive as soon as possible, another part remained wary of what awaited us. When Alma and I had taken tours of the maternity wards in three local hospitals, the nurses' enthusiasm for too many imposing machines, straps, tubes, and wires had driven us to plan for a different sort of labor, though nothing as straight up as a home birth. The memories of too many Beng women's difficult deliveries remained raw. I could still hear our neighbor Nguessan's screams in the back of our rattly Renault as we drove her from the village to the infirmary in M'Bahiakro, could remember the force of her kicks against the front seat as I tried to focus on navigating the ruts of the dirt road, could remember what a close call her baby had when finally delivered—a frail child who died only a few years later. Nguessan herself died during another delivery.

"Still three centimeters," Laura announced when they returned. Alma had an apologetic look on her face as if the low number were her fault, as if she controlled the body that racked her with pain.

We played four or five more turns, interrupted by at least as many contractions, and when the game finally ended, Alma had destroyed us both. I've always been a bum at Scrabble. This time, while I felt my usual self-castigating Why-can't-a-writer-be-better-at-word-games? I also embraced a sort of stunned pride in my wife, who came through victorious no matter how many contractions had distracted her. Alma knew how to concentrate, that was certain — one of the reasons she was such a ferocious fieldworker, able to endure all obstacles in pursuit of her research. Laura and I gave Alma high-fives (gently, gently), and all the praise that a woman in labor deserves.

We sat silently, staring at the board. Not even the Scrabble Champion was in the mood for another game. The afternoon lingered on without much change, and Laura and I took turns catching brief naps. While Laura slept, Alma and I sat together on the couch, tired and talked out, my hand holding hers, ready to be the sponge for her next squeeze. I couldn't remember life ever having been anything but my wife in labor. Still, I felt happy that we remained at home, had been able to take a walk down the block, or play Scrabble, and didn't yet have to deal with a medical staff anticipating any signs of an emergency. Sure, that was the nurses' job, but I could imagine their anxious hovering amplifying our own anxiety. Home exuded calm. Laura exuded calm.

We wouldn't have followed this path if we hadn't lived among the Beng. Still, ours was hardly a Beng experience: no dirt-floor poverty here, no threatening spirits or witchcraft, little chance our child would be born underweight and weakened prey for any lurking illness. On the other hand, our little trio was small change indeed: somewhere in Bengland right now, an infant had just been born, and the first sight she saw was a circle of her closest female relatives while nearly the entire village lined up to greet her, dozens upon dozens of new faces about to become her first experience of the world.

ALMA: TWO HOMES AND A HOSPITAL

Pacing and moaning through our house as my contractions intensified, I remembered Amenan in labor, sitting on her packed-dirt floor, leaning back slightly against her mother, legs outstretched, forehead sweating, saying to me in her fine French, "*Je souffre un peu*"—I'm suffering a little. The example of her stoicism shamed me whenever I pestered Laura, "How much longer?"

If only Laura could throw some cowry shells, Beng-style, to divine the outcome of this day. Perversely, I recalled the story of Amenan's mother getting stuck in labor for hours, before a diviner revealed that a sorcerer cousin was bewitching her; the labor only progressed once a tree fell on the cousin, vengefully sent by a protecting Earth spirit. I winced when I recalled Amenan telling me that she herself had almost died while delivering her son, Kouadio. Had my Beng friends ever lost hope, imagining they might never emerge from their ordeal, that a healthy baby would never arrive, that the witches would never be vanquished? After living so long among the Beng, I felt continually pulled back to their African reality, even in this most intense of moments when my body ought to crowd out all thoughts of elsewhere.

Finally Laura pronounced the arrival of the magical six centimeters. Excited, we gathered up our gear: reading pillows, some music tapes, a boom box to play them on, and a pair of birthing stools we'd covered with pink and white tie-dyed cloth from Côte d'Ivoire. A Beng woman would have laughed at all we toted along, but if I couldn't deliver our baby at home, I wanted to bring some chunks of home with me.

Arrived in the gleaming lobby of the hospital, the fear of losing control of my delivery formed the theme of my stay: polite but firm refusal. No, I didn't want to ride a wheelchair to the maternity ward. Once settled in a pastel-colored birthing room, I said no to being hooked up to machines, no to painkillers, no to lying down in bed. Remaining vertical—like most of the laboring women in the world—was the best way to let gravity do the work of pushing the baby down the birth canal. But the head nurse frowned at my rebuffs. She was offering the best of what her schooling and experience had assured her was the right way to have a baby. A more sympathetic young nurse-in-training offered me ice chips to suck on as I squirmed on the labor-room love seat, and furtive smiles as well as another pillow for my back.

If I were giving birth in Bengland, my husband wouldn't be with me, I'd be surrounded by my mom, a couple of aunts, maybe some older cousins, and they'd know when I should rest, what prayers to recite, who to chase away. Philip and I were just making it up as we went along, I thought, as I glanced from nurse to Laura to nurse's assistant, wondering when my doctor would arrive and how he'd react to our motley crew.

When Laura announced that I was fully dilated, the head nurse stood taller and gestured me over to the bed. Dutifully obeying through my pain, I started to trudge toward the steel-framed mattress, but Laura reminded me of the advantages of gravity in the final stages of delivery and gently suggested I try the birthing stool we'd brought along. Embarrassed, I limped over to the low seat that Laura had set in front of the small couch so Philip could sit behind me and massage my shoulders. The nurse frowned: in that position, the baby would be born onto the carpeted floor, but Laura was already spreading a clean sheet on the carpet in front of me. The nurse stared at us incredulously, but Laura—whose med-student status meant she outranked the nurse—prevailed.

Soon my obstetrician entered the room and surveyed the scene. Exhibiting the open-mindedness for which he was locally famous, he walked casually to a rocking chair in the corner of the room. Settling in to rock, he watched Philip and Laura coach me to puff and push.

≋   After Nathaniel's birth, I craved company.

No Visitors while Baby in the Room warned the sign next to the elevator on the maternity ward. But I'd seen too many African newborns passed from person to person to believe that healthy adults imperiled healthy babies just by holding them. My first afternoon in the hospital, I called a friend. "I'd love you to come by."

"Really? Aren't you tired?"

"Sure, a little," I answered. "But, well, you can hold the baby—he's so adorable, he looks straight at you!"

"Okay, I'll come after work today." She hesitated. "Will they let me in your room?"

"If you stop by around 5:30, I think you can sneak in," I calculated. "That's when they're busy serving dinner. Just walk down the hall like you belong."

Thus began Nathaniel's illegal welcoming committee, a steady line of guests that continued a day later when we brought him home.

By his fourth day in his new crib, Nathaniel scrunched up his face and bellowed a baby misery we couldn't interpret. Our parenting books dispensed plenty of advice—starting with putting our newborn on a schedule. But Nathaniel clearly hadn't read the books and wanted none of their timetables. If the schedule didn't work, their last resort for advice was: Listen to my maternal instinct. Some help!

Struggling to manage the seemingly endless cascade of our new son's tears, Philip and I cast about in our memories of West African villages, crowded with infants and young children. *Did Beng infants cry so much? And if so, what would a parent do?* Recalling village life, I pictured a mother packing a crying baby onto her back for the day, tucked tightly into a *pagne* cloth wrapped around her middle. Perhaps Nathaniel might enjoy that, too. I scoured our pile of baby-shower presents and found a padded cloth frontpack still in its box. Straining with complicated straps and buckles, I stuffed wiggly limbs through the small leg holes; as soon as the zipper closed him in tight, Nathaniel quieted down.

It seemed a miracle: as long as he cozied up in there, he stayed content. From afar, Beng mothers had offered good advice.

Walking Nathaniel for hours around the neighborhood, warm against my chest, I suspected I had much more to learn from my West African friends. During my previous field trips, I'd studied other aspects of women's lives—especially their lives as wives and sisters—yet, not a mother myself, I'd neglected to pay much systematic attention to their lives as mothers. I had no idea how often Beng women breastfed or when they introduced solid foods to their babies, nor did I know if Beng babies walked or talked on the same schedule that American babies do. I'd prided myself on my skills as a researcher, but how could I possibly understand African women's lives without taking into account their experiences as mothers?

Censored Words

MARCH 1990

PHILIP: *LA CRISE*

The driver from the American Cultural Center chatted up the schedule details for Côte d'Ivoire's first writers' conference, treating me with whatever deference he thought was due to a "Distinguished American Guest." I still had trouble believing that mouthful of a title referred to me and only mustered a half-listen, tired from the international flight, worried how well I'd manage with my bum French, and trying to take in the names of all the writers Blé was reeling off: Jérôme Carlos, Tanella Boni, Jean-Marie Adiaffi . . .

The names came and went as I basked in the familiar humid heat and punishing sun of Africa after a five-year absence. How strange, though, to arrive in Côte d'Ivoire alone, while Alma stayed home with Nathaniel. Even though I'd be here only ten days, we'd decided our nearly three-year-old son was still too young for the health risks of a tropical climate. Blé crossed the bridge that led from the airport to the downtown neighborhoods of Marcory and Treichville, and I straightened up at the sight of blocks of stores with smashed windows. While women walked by balancing on their heads baskets filled with yams, or fruit, or cloth, and young men hawked sunglasses and watches to passing traffic, clusters of soldiers parked at every main thoroughfare, silently daring any new trouble.

"My god, would you look at that," I murmured. So this was what Ivorians dubbed *La Crise*—The Crisis. In the States, I'd followed news reports that protests against the government had spread throughout the capital in recent weeks. Here was my first look at some of the damage. I'd often wondered how long Ivorians would maintain their patience with the government's klepto-culture. It took the aging President Houphouët-Boigny's self-indulgent construction of the world's largest cathedral in his small hometown of Yamoussoukro to set his country on a simmer. This discontent was compounded by the real economic hardship that had come to Côte d'Ivoire in the past year when the international price for coffee—one of the country's main exports—had fallen by 50 percent. When the president reacted to the public outcry by claiming that he was simply donating $180 million of his "private funds" to the project, resentment flipped to outrage, and then demonstrations flipped to violence. Blé drove us past more shattered storefronts, more groups of idling military. Little wonder a mere literary conference had almost been canceled.

≋ The first sessions of the conference took place at an ocean resort in the nearby town of Grand Bassam, the former colonial capital of Côte d'Ivoire. Behind us stood the neglected mansions of the town's heyday, and before us stretched the long swaying leaves of palm trees, the pervasive crash of surf on the beach, and bare-breasted French tourists strolling to the water's edge.

Our conference might have seemed far from the country's troubles, except for the occasional sight of gaunt children begging for coins, the presence of gendarmes patrolling the paths along the beach, and the writers who took the opportunity to let loose long bottled-up words. The novelist Jérôme Carlos delivered a keynote speech critiquing West African society that everyone understood was a critique of Ivorian society in specific: the crisis of poor schools, the oppression of single-party rule, and the excessive influence of the military. Tanella Boni addressed the country's miserable record on women's rights, while the poet and playwright Jean-Marie Adiaffi, a raffish sort who seemed to acknowledge no inhibition, railed about everything under the sun. Presiding serenely over the airing of ills sat a white-haired Bernard Dadié, considered the father of Ivorian literature—and admired by everyone because he'd quit his post as minister of culture over the regime's corruption.

Later that afternoon, during the taping of a radio interview about the conference's first day, the dapper Jérôme Carlos answered an unpromising question about the role of literature with an impassioned speech, while Tiburce Koffi added verbal sparks of his own, and a gleeful Jean-Marie Adiaffi egged them on. The two men grew more enraged as they spoke, and I began to worry about what sort of reaction they might be courting.

The interviewer stopped listening—his tight frown announcing better than words that none of this could possibly be broadcast. These writers were simply making his job more difficult. Finally he turned to me, hoping to salvage his assignment. "Is literature necessarily political?" he asked.

"Of course," I answered, grateful for the opportunity to support Jérôme and Tiburce, "every writer has to follow a vision, even if it contradicts the current dogma of the day, whatever that dogma might be—religious, scientific, social, political." Before I finished speaking, I already blushed at my pomposity—I'd borrowed a touch too much of my new friends' high-flying rhetoric.

The interviewer sighed, thanked us sarcastically, and packed up his equipment.

≋ I sat by the bedside in my hotel room back in Abidjan the following morning and clicked on the radio on the fat chance that our interview would be broadcast. Sipping room-service coffee through a news and entertainment show full of rapid-fire Ivorian French and the latest shimmering dance music, I finally heard my name announced, and there was my voice speaking English in the background of the announcer's translation. As I'd expected, my words and most of the rest of the radio interview had been censored, except for an innocuous sliver of my general praise for the conference. This muzzling was nothing new for my friends at the conference, but it was a first for me; I couldn't discount the thought that one of the reasons Jérôme and Tiburce had pushed the envelope yesterday was for me to experience this too.

An exhilarating feeling, that my words could frighten someone in power enough to suppress them. Before I could ease too much into smug self-regard, I reminded myself that this was all a kind of game. The writers and reporters knew each other well, had gone to school together. Last month, many of the journalists now at the conference had watched from their offices as an angry crowd had threatened to burn down the headquarters of the country's official—and only—newspaper, *Fraternité Matin*. In the break between sessions yesterday, they'd joked about the ironies of agreeing with a mob that had threatened their lives. But as employees of the state-run media, they couldn't write honestly about the political situation. Still, they found ways to sidestep the blackout on the country's political opposition. Last night's television news reported the upheavals in Eastern Europe and the Soviet Union—the Latvian declaration of independence, the East German elections—seemingly distant protests against single-party rule.

Clicking off the radio, I prepared for another day at the conference. When the sessions resumed later in the morning, I realized just how much events in Europe inspired the imaginations of the writers. Though I'd arrived in Abidjan just two weeks after the release of Nelson Mandela from prison, no one mentioned him, not even Jérôme Carlos, who was the author of a novel titled *Les Infants de Mandela*. Instead, Carlos read a poem in the conference's afternoon session about the African as a statue whose limbs need to come alive, just as similar statues had animated themselves in Poland, Czechoslovakia, and Hungary.

One of the reasons I'd been invited to the conference was an essay I'd published a year before, "A Writer in a World of Spirits," which recounted some of my village experiences among the Beng—consulting a diviner for writer's block, attempting to translate one of my short stories at a storytelling session, searching for a space to write while living in a culture that has no word for privacy. At a panel devoted to this essay, I read from selections that had been translated into a better French than my pronunciation deserved. With the exception of Bernard Dadié, whose autobiographical novel *Climbié* recounted his village childhood, these urban Ivorian writers seemed embarrassed by their distance from my essay's details of African rural life. For them, the village was the past, Abidjan's modernity the future.

I realized I'd heard little said about the plight of the country's rural poor. Whenever I mentioned village concerns, the writers and reporters offered supportive lip service and moved on, or they simply gazed at me, as if the thought had never occurred to them. Apparently, the political crisis consuming them was a local dispute, city trouble that ignored the lives of villagers throughout the country. I welcomed the idea of political change too, but I began to question what, if anything, it would achieve for the Beng.

ALMA: CAN YOU TEACH ANTHROPOLOGY TO A TODDLER?

Nathaniel ran ahead of me down the sidewalk, and I called out, "Hey, not so fast!"

He slowed down . . . then caught sight of a robin pecking for worms on our neighbor's front yard. Cautiously, he approached until the bird flitted away. The cool breeze of this March day signaled another few weeks of not-yet-spring before new grass would crowd out brown stubble. Still, our neighbors might not appreciate our son walking on their incipient lawn.

"We need to stay on the sidewalk, honey," I said, too tired to keep up with him. I hadn't slept much after yesterday's phone call from Philip in Abidjan. He'd told me that, as he was about to go out with a group of writers to see a play, a friend announced that a colleague had just called, warning of police blockading the roads and searching cars for anti-government flyers. Although I'd marveled at the thought of samizdat being passed around Abidjan, I couldn't stop worrying when Philip also mentioned that a radio interview he'd joined with some of the Ivorian writers had been censored by the government. Tomorrow he'd be walking about Abidjan with Bertin, a Beng university student who was the son of our former Kosangbé hosts, François and Makola, and though Philip promised to be careful about where he would travel, it was hard for him to suppress the excitement in his voice. While the anthropologist in me reveled in the news of Côte d'Ivoire's exciting transformation, the mother in me worried how I could possibly return with a child to a country in turmoil.

Again Nathaniel wandered onto another neighbor's lawn. In a Beng village it's perfectly acceptable to tromp through another family's courtyard on the way to somewhere else, as long as you engage in elaborate greetings as you pass through. But we weren't living in a Beng village.

"Sweetie," I called out again, tiring from his toddler's energy, "we need to keep off the yards."

Nathaniel looked at me with questioning eyes. "Why?"

I hesitated. "These yards belong to other people," I began, trying to translate from a lecture that I'd given my students recently about the cultural values lurking in American suburbs. "You know how you don't like it if another child takes one of your toys and doesn't want to give it back?"

Nathaniel nodded.

"It's kind of like that with lawns."

"But I'm not *taking* the lawn," he replied, in that precocious voice of his.

"True," I said. "But, well, it's theirs. They don't like to share it."

"Then they're selfish," Nathaniel said.

Suppressing a smile, I tried another tactic. "You see how the sidewalk goes in a straight line?"

Nathaniel eyed the neatly aligned blocks and nodded.

"Well, they're like that so we'll walk in a straight line too."

Nathaniel frowned, and tried his best. But he kept making his own zigzag line on the cement sidewalk as if, although he didn't know it, his feet led him down a Beng path.

≋ After returning home, Nathaniel settled into a rare nap that I knew wouldn't last long, so I set to work at my desk.

Philip's article about his life as a writer in Africa had generated interest from publishers, and now we had a contract to write a book about our time among the Beng. The mad intensity of those times had percolated for ten years, yet I still wasn't sure how best to tell our story. Already we'd decided to alternate our voices as we moved the narrative forward, but what worried me most was the thought of telling stories that I'd rather not reveal—not only about the Beng, but also about myself. I'd made so many embarrassing errors in my first months of fieldwork.

I stared at the computer screen, stuck. How to recount my disastrous attempt to take a census a scant week after moving into a tiny Beng village? One woman claimed not to know the names of her children, another declined to name her husband, and a third claimed ignorance of her own name. Though I learned much later why the villagers had been so suspicious of my intentions, how could I allow myself to appear so hopelessly naïve?

The title Philip and I had chosen for our book, *Parallel Worlds*, was perhaps too apt. At times in the village I'd despaired of ever feeling the elusive, mystical Rapport that was the prize of every anthropologist's dream. The lines of our worlds, no matter how closely they approached each other, always felt parallel.

Would they always? Certainly Beng values had complicated my notions of child rearing. And since becoming a mother, I'd been accumulating a host of questions on note cards that I'd never asked the Beng women whose lives I'd thought I understood. I hoped to ask them some day, as the subject of my next fieldwork project. Philip and I were already planning on a family return to Côte d'Ivoire, when Nathaniel was older.

PHILIP: OUR OWN HOUSE OF *MBARI*

Children sped back and forth in a dirt alley, scuffling after a soccer ball—a common enough sight in an Abidjan neighborhood, but what they shouted weren't cries of team support. "Houphouët, *voleur!* Houphouët, *voleur!*"

I almost laughed at such a previously unheard-of scene; back in 1980, because of the prosperity he'd brought to the country, Houphouët-Boigny had been regarded as a near-god by Ivorians. Now, even kids called him a thief.

Beside me Bertin clicked his tongue, a comment on what Côte d'Ivoire had come to. With the literary conference on hiatus for the next couple of days, for most of the afternoon Bertin and I had been ranging about Abidjan, walking past heaps of garbage that hadn't been collected because of the unrest, on too many streets that still showed the effects of violent protest—even banks had their windows smashed.

Bertin had a lot of time on his hands too, since the government had closed down the university during the protests. Because his parents were poor farmers, Alma and I had helped support him through his high school studies. Now he was in his first year at the national university, though if the school shutdown continued, he'd likely have to start from scratch in the fall.

I knew Bertin mainly from the letters he sent us, thanking us for our support and passing on the increasingly bleak village news of drought and crop failure. Unlike François, his chatty father, Bertin appeared to be a cautious fellow. His English and my French were about on a par, so as we ambled about the city we spoke in an awkward mix of the two, his silences occasionally broken by a quirky burst of what almost sounded like apologetic laughter. To my relief he seemed a trustworthy soul. I'd decided to cash out the bulk of my honorarium from the conference, split it into parcels, and send them up-country to Amenan, Yacouba, and a few other families. But how to accomplish this? Bertin might just be the right man for the job.

≋ I woke to the phone ringing and reached for it, anticipating a call from Alma, hoping to hear her voice, and then Nathaniel's. I missed them terribly. But when I picked up the receiver, an unfamiliar voice on the other end invited me to a meeting with the American ambassador to Côte d'Ivoire for that afternoon. I masked my surprise while accepting the invitation. Most of my official dealings had been with staff at the American Cultural Center, not the embassy. The ambassador must have a lot of time on his hands, I thought, if he could request a meeting at such short notice.

After breakfast I settled at my hotel room's small desk to work away at the manuscript of the book Alma and I had begun on our life among the Beng. There were some areas I wouldn't mind avoiding. How could I write about barging into the secrecy of a cult's religious ceremony, or the arguments we'd had with Jean, Alma's failed field assistant? For the rest of the morning I wallowed in embarrassing stories I'd prefer to forget.

The embassy was parked around the corner from my hotel, lined with sturdy concrete pylons on the sidewalk. The sight reminded me of our old friends from the embassy, Al and Esti Votaw, who befriended Alma and me in our earliest days in Côte d'Ivoire and fed our scrawny selves whenever we visited Abidjan after a few months of village living. Years later, Al was reassigned to Lebanon where, six days after his arrival, he died in the Beirut embassy bombing. I remembered turning my gaze from the newspaper photos of the blasted building, afraid I might recognize my friend's body. Now, as I offered my passport to the marine sitting behind a glass window thick enough to deflect bullets, even a bomb, I offered Al silent thanks for his friendship.

The ambassador's office was crisp and clean, and the air conditioner purred with such a particularly American intensity that I could almost imagine I wasn't in Africa. The man himself sported a neatly tailored look, suitable for the daily requirements of ambassadorial such-and-such. We began with small talk about the conference, my experiences living in small villages in the country. I found myself flattered but also a bit surprised that he knew so much about me.

"So, what do the, ah . . . is it the Beng?"

I nodded.

"What do the, um, the Beng think about the political situation?"

"Well," I said, "I haven't met anyone from any ethnic group who defends the president."

Now it was his turn to nod. "Well, if you hear or see anything interesting, I'd be happy to listen to whatever you have to say."

Usually, I considered myself an accommodating person, willing—too often, I sometimes worried—to offer the benefit of the doubt. But I hadn't come to Côte d'Ivoire to be anyone's spy. In any awkward pause like this I usually found myself jumping in to fill the silence. "I'm just here to participate in a literary conference. I'm sure there are people at the embassy who are better at that than I could ever be," I replied, despising myself for trying to smooth over my refusal. But this was, after all, a diplomatic situation, and it called for a diplomatic response.

"Sure, I understand," he said, in a voice that surely disguised his thoughts too, and within minutes our little meeting was over.

Hoping to shake that exchange out of my head, I hailed a cab and headed for the Hotel Ivoire, the country's pricy tourist mecca that boasted a bowling alley, skating rink, movie theater, and ice cream parlor. All I wanted was to sit in the spacious lobby, order a drink, or maybe an ice cream, and watch the local and foreign rich go about their business, as if nothing potentially explosive was brewing outside.

In the lobby luxurious with marble, polished wood, and wide glass windows overlooking the lagoon and Abidjan's skyline, I found myself wandering toward the bookstore of the hotel's slick commercial promenade. After days of listening to conference talks presented in French, and conducting conversations in my imperfect command of the language, I'd grown hungry for my own language, so I picked up a small stack of English-language African news magazines. Then I laid claim to a soft upholstered chair in the lobby.

Paging my way from one issue to another, I read that dissent seemed to brew everywhere—in Gabon, Niger, Zambia. In Kenya, angry clerics were using the pulpit to denounce the country's one-party system. In Ghana, a popular soccer player had been suspended after refusing to shake hands with the president-via-coup, Jerry Rawlings, during a team lineup.

Nestled among all the accounts of unusual upheaval was an excerpt from a lecture that the Nigerian novelist Chinua Achebe had recently presented in Great Britain. Achebe described a ritual celebration performed by his ethnic group, the Igbo. From time to time the earth goddess, Ana, would announce to diviners that an mbari house needed to be built, and the chosen artisans would fill it up with sculptures and murals to depict, in Achebe's words, "the entire kingdom of human experience and imagination." An mbari house allows every sort of art, from scenes of daily life to evocations of the fantastic, the unapologetically sexual, the abnormal. I was struck by the wisdom of this essential metaphor for art: a house that contains within it every possibility, nothing off limits. Here, perhaps, was the key Alma and I had been seeking. We still struggled with just what to include—or not—in our memoir, but a polite book wasn't worth writing. So what if Alma had made some mistakes in the field? All anthropologists did, and I'd made a fool of myself more than once. If we were going to reveal secrets of Beng village life, we shouldn't be hoarding any of our own. How would Alma and I manage this?

Back in the Village

MAY – JUNE 1993

ALMA: THE HOUSE OF AFRICA

Hours had passed since the airplane cabin's lights dimmed; still, as midnight came and went, our son's eyes refused to shut. Nathaniel squirmed first one way then another, searching for a comfortable fit between Philip and me; no doubt he sensed the extra energy radiating from us, our moods careening between excitement and anxiety. How could I be hauling my son to a place that swarmed with tropical parasites, viruses, and bacteria?

Months ago, when Philip and I first sat him down on the comfortable blue couch in our living room and warned him of the eight shots and boosters he'd need, Nathaniel had flashed a look of dismay, then eased into a faraway look and asked, "Can't we just stand outside the house of Africa and look in the window?"

Philip and I realized our child had no idea what his parents were planning. Yet Africa was central to who Philip and I had become, and we wanted our son to join that part of our lives—and join the extended village family that had accepted us. So we hoped our perpetually curious six-year-old child—pleading "More things!" was how Nathaniel often greeted the end of any picture book we'd read him when a toddler—would thrive in the More Things of a different culture.

Now, as Nathaniel leaned his head against my shoulder, I glanced at the book on my lap. Printed just weeks before we'd left the United States, the memoir Philip and I had labored over for more than three years was about to reach the land that had inspired it. I hoped it might—just might—help improve the lives of the people it described.

Having built a career around my research among the Beng, and having my inner life expanded by their cultural perspective, I felt I owed a debt I could never fully repay. Many anthropologists believed that the time for temporary reciprocity was gone, that even a lifelong commitment to a field community was morally required. Indeed, Philip and I had vowed that if we were ever in the position to offer ongoing support to the Beng, we would. From becoming enmeshed in kinship ties that began as fictive but soon felt real enough, we had come to understand the Beng value that in families, everything—not only bounty and good fortune but even illness and misfortune—should be shared. And so, while revising our text, we had also re-envisioned our ethical relations with the community that continued to host us, and we planned to donate the advance for *Parallel Worlds* to the two Beng villages where we'd lived. We hoped our effort wouldn't turn into yet another disappointing development project gone wrong.

"Tea or coffee?" The flight attendant pushed her cart and roused dozing passengers for cold croissants and beverages of our choice. My Jewish mother's nightmare moment had arrived: Food or sleep? I opted against rest and nudged Nathaniel awake. Once in a remote village in the rain forest, keeping him well nourished could prove a challenge; a few extra calories now might come in handy later.

Across the aisle, a little girl with plaited hair sucked on an orange slice. Over dinner last night, she'd offered Nathaniel one of the chocolates on her tray, but he'd declined her gesture of friendship—perhaps made shy by her unexpected French, compounded by the African passengers around us wearing brightly colored fabrics, and chatting in languages he didn't understand.

Could Nathaniel make friends in the village, or would he be overwhelmed by the gatherings of curious children sure to encircle him? Sure, we'd brought along a hefty bag of Legos, but they would hardly compensate for his missing his friends back home.

Through the window of our plane, Abidjan sprawled below. Cars sped along the curved shoreline of the Cornice highway, past office-building complexes, over modern bridges spanning the lagoon. I could already imagine the pungent aroma of spicy brochettes grilling on outdoor braziers, the sweet ripeness bursting from the mango trees that lined so many city sidewalks.

"*Bienvenus à Côte d'Ivoire*," the pilot welcomed us as we touched down.

Hurrahs rose from the returning Ivorians. Philip sighed, perhaps thinking of his father, ill and now an ocean away.

"I'll get our stuff," Philip murmured, collecting two briefcases, a video camera case, three backpacks. As I rose to help, it seemed much easier to keep track of these bags than of our worries.

After we made our way through customs, a droopy Nathaniel perked up when we stepped outside into a steamy tropical morning.

"So, what do you think, sweetie?" I asked.

Nathaniel hesitated a moment as he looked beyond the terminal to the rushing traffic leading off to a city skyline. "This is not what I expected."

"Oh?" Philip shot me an amused look, then addressed Nathaniel. "What do you mean?"

"I thought . . . it . . . wouldn't be so modern."

"Ah," I nodded, appalled that I had committed the anthropological sin of overemphasizing the exotic in favor of the familiar. Philip and I had spent so much time describing village life to Nathaniel, we'd neglected to mention that we'd spend our first weeks in a large city.

The city was indeed where we were bound. Making our way through the gauntlet of teenage boys competing for the prize of carrying our bags in return for a tip, we spotted the driver from the American embassy and loaded everything into his black sedan. Maybe we'd recapture our energy after a long nap in the hotel.

PHILIP: RAISING THE STAKES

Refreshed from our naps, we peered out from the taxi windows at the dark Abidjan streets, on our way to the neighborhood of Yopougon, which included a small *quartier* of Beng. Nathaniel sat between us in the back, taking in his first sights of African nightlife: women selling roasted corn beneath the lush crowns of slender palm trees; mounds of garbage piled by the roadside; coughing, overpacked buses; women balancing on their heads remarkable amounts of patterned cloth or firewood, ceramic bowls or towers of yams; young girls hawking clear plastic bags of *yi glacé*—cold water. I could still remember my own first look at night in this city, as if all the African novels I'd read had burst into three-dimensional color in the humid heat; now I wondered what my six-year-old son saw. The "house of Africa" must certainly look larger than he'd imagined.

Everywhere, men and women walked in restless intent to who knows what destinations, and our cab driver pointed them out with a chuckle. He called them *les onzes*—the elevens—and then explained the nickname: people who were too poor to afford a bus ticket or a taxi ride, or own a bicycle, could get around only on their two legs, which resembled the paired digits of the number 11. I kept my thoughts to myself about the cabbie's cruel humor. Even Bertin, after years of schooling and university study, teetered on the verge of *les onzes* poverty: if Alma hadn't offered him a job as a field assistant for this summer, he might have had to work the city intersections, hawking sunglasses or flip-flops to drivers idling at stoplights. Côte d'Ivoire may have fought for the right to multiparty elections, but decades of governmental mismanagement and corruption seemed to be finally catching up with it.

Far from the glitz of downtown Abidjan, the cab driver dropped us off at a market's edge. A maze of stalls, cobbled together with scrap wood, overlapping chunks of recycled corrugated tin sheets, strips of linoleum, and curtains fashioned from faded old *pagnes*, sprawled into the distance. Kiosks displayed dozens of local newspapers, some of them as basic as a single broadsheet—a choice of opinion reflecting both the new multiparty political reality brought about by the protests of three years ago, and a growing political maturity that might serve the country well when the ailing president, Houphouët-Boigny, would eventually pass away.

Food stands and *maquis*—open-air bars—blared competing music tapes into the night air, one heady dance tune with chirping, skipping guitars slowly giving way to another. We walked through these shifting soundscapes among ragged peddlers and prostitutes form-fitted into the tightest of dresses—in this era of AIDS they were beautiful bombs waiting to go off, and certainly more than a few of the men we passed could be harboring the disease as well. Earlier in the day I'd turned on the hotel-room television in search of CNN but instead came upon the middle of a public service report on AIDS: a woman demonstrated proper condom application by slipping one over an appropriately long and curved banana. Alma distracted Nathaniel from the screen, but I'd stood there, amazed at a sight that, eight years ago, would have been impossible, when condoms were illegal and the Ivorian government denied that AIDS was a problem. Now the country had the highest rate of the disease in West Africa. Alma and I had brought along a box of hundreds of condoms to dispense in the village, donated back home by a local NGO, yet how could this be little more than an inadequate gesture?

We passed a man grilling bush meat and took in the smoky, slightly acrid tang in the air. Nathaniel slowed at the sight of the splayed bodies of squirrels and hamster-like *agouti* sizzling on a wire mesh above an old oil drum, but he kept his opinions to himself. I didn't dare mention that we'd likely be eating similar meals once we landed in the village—a notoriously picky eater, Nathaniel had once refused everything but cottage cheese for months.

We came upon a clutch of young men crowded around a foosball table. Out of a habitual gesture of respect, two fellows in tattered T-shirts made way for us, but before Alma or I could excuse ourselves from this little drama of un-earned privilege, Nathaniel accepted the empty space. He'd never seen a soccer game before, much less this domesticated version, and he couldn't peel his eyes away from the fast-paced action: the tiny ball ripping back and forth, the twists and turns of the two players' bodies as they manipulated the game table's long metal bars attached to stiff, paint-chipped figures serving as rival teams. Alma and I stood beside our son and watched one game, then another.

"*Le petit chef, il aime le baby fut,*" someone observed, and the crowd murmured amused approval. Nathaniel's attention, though, was more likely focused on the construction of the table and the placement of the metal bars, as if the game's mechanics were a puzzle to be deciphered.

Only a tug on his hand could tear him away, but a few makeshift stalls later we came upon another game of *le baby fut*. Alma and I decided to honor Nathaniel's enthusiasm and wait another day to search out the Beng *quartier*; instead, we made our way through the market from one foosball game to another, accompanied by the competing chiming guitars of popular songs.

≋   The following morning we hauled ourselves through the heat to the American embassy for the necessary presentation of passports, since the National Endowment for the Humanities had funded part of Alma's research. The cab dropped us off at the entrance to the street, which was blocked to through traffic. So we walked to an embassy that now resembled a fortress, ringed by much larger protective concrete pylons than the ones I'd noted back in 1990.

Past the marines guarding the gated entrance, we were politely but thoroughly frisked by security. Then we made our way through a few offices, explaining Alma's work as she filled out various forms. When she mentioned that we intended to donate half the royalties of our memoir of Africa to the two Beng villages where we'd lived, one official paused in his paperwork.

"Really? You should speak with Barbara Brown. She oversees development grants for small villages. I'm sure she'd like to meet you. Here, let me ring her up."

Within minutes we were sitting in her sparsely decorated office, Nathaniel kneeling in a corner with his Legos spread out before him. A handsome woman, broad-shouldered and open-faced, Barbara Brown gave off an air of formality, but I could see she could barely contain her pleasure when we told her our plans.

We soon realized why, when she offered to contribute development money to our royalty funds. The U.S. embassy had a new matching-grant program meant to support small-scale, locally appropriate village projects.

"It's hard, though," she said, "to find the right contact person in a village, someone local who won't end up stealing the money. If you decide with the villagers on a project that would meet our guidelines, we could add anywhere from 50 percent to 75 percent to your funds."

Alma and I couldn't stop sharing grins as we spoke to Barbara. While we were insiders who could likely ensure success and up her program's average on what so far seemed to have been a spotty record, with the help of her grant aid our royalties could multiply their effectiveness. But hadn't the stakes for success just been raised? I couldn't help recalling the innumerable contentious meetings we'd sat through in the village of Kosangbé, and my doubts returned that they'd ever come to a consensus about anything, though for the moment I kept those doubts to myself. Alma wasn't voicing any concerns either. No need to unduly worry this woman we'd just met.

Nathaniel continued building what at first I thought were towers but which eventually revealed themselves as versions of the concrete pylons outside the embassy. I let out a silent sigh, remembering Al Votaw, who once worked down the hall in a nearby office, and I imagined him peeking his head in the doorway, with his long hair and large ungainly mustache. We hadn't mentioned his death in *Parallel Worlds*, wanting to afford his family some privacy, but the absence of that truth now gnawed at me. One day, perhaps, we'd give him his due. Alma touched my arm. Barbara Brown regarded me, apparently waiting for an answer to whatever question she'd just posed, and I had to ask her to repeat what she'd said.

"How does a married couple manage to write a book together and stay married?"

I hesitated. This was a question we'd been asked dozens of times, and Alma and I hadn't yet come up with a pat answer.

"Oh, we had our moments," Alma prompted, flashing me a look that reminded me she still worked on forgiving the annoying mantra of my editorial comments: *Needs narrative tension* or the much worse NQR—shorthand for *Not quite right*. We'd wrestled over conflicting memories, negotiated what to leave out and what to keep. Once, stung by a particularly tactless comment, Alma had barged out of the house, declaring, "I'm taking a walk—by *myself*. Don't bother to follow." Chastened, I gave her five minutes before I drove up and down nearby streets until I pulled alongside her with an apology and a suggestion that we take a break and catch a movie. A comedy seemed in order, and we chose *City Slickers*, which turned out to be such a ramshackle affair of predictable gags that we left in the middle, oddly invigorated and laughing—finally!—to ourselves that we could do better than *that*.

Now I smiled at Barbara and said, "Patience and forgiveness." Somehow we'd managed to remain partners, not rivals, in the writing that consumed us for nearly three years. Our growing book had become another version of the difficult fieldwork that we struggled to describe, and we had to work together to conjure the necessary words to complete it.

≋　I woke early that morning beside Alma in our hotel room, absorbing the shock of finding myself far from home, even if Côte d'Ivoire was home too. Over the years, the belief system and cultural assumptions that lived so vividly within our village neighbors had helped me slowly learn a local common sense that wasn't immediately obvious to an outsider. I'd realized how much of culture is invisible, that the things of the material world are mere whitecaps on an unseen, arcing wave. When I trained that vision on the culture I grew up with, then the invisible of home began to coalesce, a gift of sight that influenced my writing. I glanced over at Nathaniel lying on the neighboring bed, curled up beneath the sheet, his sleeping face half hidden by a pillow. This summer would shape him as well, but in what ways?

I closed my eyes, though sleep was long gone—not because of the heat and bright morning light radiating through the curtains, or the sound of traffic, but because I couldn't resist the emotional tug of Gloria Naylor's *Mama Day*, a novel I'd brought with me that was set on a Georgia sea island and steeped in a local magic with an African pedigree.

Soon we'd begin our preparations for the day, including the negotiations for the summer's rental of a car, through Ben Assida, an old high school teacher of Bertin who'd given up teaching a few years back to go into shipping, then expanded his business to include a garage with a stable of mechanics. Surely Ben wouldn't rent us a lemon.

While Alma and Nathaniel still slept, I reached for the book on the night table, tucking into the last chapters as quietly as possible until the loss and revelations of the end undid me: first a hint of tears and then, to my alarmed surprise, a sobbing I struggled to silence.

Alma rustled beside me, then woke, and I managed to explain that one of the characters had died but shouldn't have; it was so unfair, so sad. Alma tried her best to comfort me out of a sadness that had lurked silently within, waiting for its moment. Nathaniel, remarkably, still slept in the bed beside us.

Questioning my own misery even as it unfolded, I suspected this pent-up emotion poured out for my father. Back in America, he continued a fight against cancer, had been doing so for a year; for all that time I couldn't admit what I most feared. During my last visit with him, even my last phone call before flying to Côte d'Ivoire, I wouldn't allow myself to delve into any subject that might lead to some version of final words. If I hadn't convinced myself I'd see him again at the end of the summer, I wouldn't have traveled thousands of miles away to the "house of Africa." And yet, though Alma's soothing voice quieted me, I couldn't shake the image of my father's weary face.

Long ago I'd learned what to wear in a small village: long wraparound skirt with matching blouse. I'd learned how to eat: lop off bits of dough with my first three fingers, dip them delicately into the fiery hot sauce. I'd learned how to greet: intone a lengthy, formulaic greeting to everyone I passed, use a kinship term that assumed we were somehow related. Here in the crowded, working-class neighborhood of Yopougon, I wished I'd worn a patterned outfit that could match the colorful *pagnes* surrounding me, instead of my beige skirt and blouse.

This meeting of the Association of Beng Youth held in the urban courtyard of Pierre, a middle-class Beng man, was less familiar territory for me as a researcher. The electric bulbs that dangled from raised wires crisscrossing the compound would bathe the courtyard in a soft glow once afternoon gave way to dusk. But when I heard the explosive *gb*'s and *kp*'s of Beng replacing the rapid-fire Africanized French of Abidjan, and the long ritual greetings as friends and family met, Abidjan's skyscrapers, ice cream parlors, and four-star hotels across town began to feel a world away. Thankfully, I struggled less to follow these speeches than I'd feared, perhaps because in recent years I'd been working with a linguistics student to assemble the first Beng-English dictionary. Lists of the Beng verbs and pronoun conjugation rules I'd labored over during our first stay so crowded my mind that sometimes my Illinois dreams came out in Beng.

Three older men enjoyed the shade of a kapok tree, settling into their folding chairs so solidly, they might have sat on thrones. Although they sported only a few strands of gray hair, their seats of honor suggested village elders deciding when to hold the next sacrifice for rain. But instead of an elder, none other than Bertin prepared to open the meeting. Sporting a neat polo shirt and tailored trousers, he clearly enjoyed some prestige as a university student. Earlier, he'd pointed out to me several college students in the crowd, and far more high school and junior high students, gossiping in small groups as only teenagers can do. Then, young as he was, Bertin announced everyone in the courtyard, concluding with *Amwé* and *Kouadio*—my Beng name and Philip's—and he read from a written agenda. Once again, village practices receded into the background.

This picking and choosing from rural and urban ways seemed to be the *modus vivendi* of the Beng students in the courtyard, and why not? Though the Beng people were a tiny, isolated ethnic group in Côte d'Ivoire, these students had spent their recent years here in the nation's economic capital and could take what they liked of city pleasures and couple them with village ways. My rural memories needed to catch up.

As the meeting continued, Nathaniel squirmed on Philip's lap.

"I'll take him around," Philip volunteered, and they left the tree's shade to explore the compound.

"It's time to collect dues," Bertin declared.

One of his companions moved from group to group to gather contributions. As he finished his rounds, he approached me and asked in French, "Would you like to join the association?"

Had I really been accepted so easily into this group of urban Beng? Many years and miles away, our first village-mates had suspected Philip and me alternately of witchcraft, spying, missionizing, being ghostly apparitions or even an incestuous brother and sister. Enticing some of the more recalcitrant elders just to respond to my *hellos* had taken months.

"Yes, of course," I said, offering our share of CFAs. I asked what the group planned to do with the money they collected.

One of the students said, "It's for some projects up in the villages."

"Ah, *bon?*"

"The villages are really in need of development," he continued. "There's still no electricity, the water pumps are old, few villages even have elementary schools . . . there's so much we need to do."

"And you can raise enough money for big projects like these?"

"We now have 160 Beng working in Abidjan and two nearby towns. Every year, they contribute 10,000 CFA each for a village project. So you see, it can really add up."

Ever since the international collapse of coffee prices four years ago, I'd worried how global economic forces might affect the many coffee farmers we knew in Beng villages. Times were hard, I knew from letters I'd received from Amenan, yet these city Beng were doing their best to help their up-country relatives.

The student moved on, and then Bertin approached, at his side a young man with closely cropped hair. "*Grande Soeur*, I want to introduce you to my friend Augustin, another student at the university." After the standard ritualized greetings, Bertin added, "Augustin's studying German."

When Bertin had agreed to work as my research assistant *au village*, I worried how he would fare. I planned to tape most of my interviews in Beng, and Bertin would need to sit at a table for hours a day, listening to my interview tapes and writing out what he heard, using a phonetic alphabet I hadn't yet taught him.

After having left his home village at the age of six to attend school—Nathaniel's age now, I realized with a pang—Bertin had never lived *en brousse* for more than a few weeks at a time. Why not hire Augustin to join him? As friends, perhaps Bertin and Augustin could keep each other company, and two assistants would increase the chances that all my tapes were typed up.

"Has Bertin told you that I'll be doing research up-country?" I asked Augustin.

"*Oui, oui.*"

I calculated silently, decided I had enough funds, and offered Augustin the job.

"*Merci,*" Augustin said quietly, shaking my hand. We agreed to talk about the details later, after I found Nathaniel and Philip.

"I saw them go into Pierre's house," Bertin said, pointing across the court-yard to a small building.

I walked over, and through the doorway I saw why Nathaniel hadn't returned to the kapok tree. "Look, Mommy, I found Legos," Nathaniel announced, lean-ing over a table and happily snapping plastic bricks into place. He worked in-tently with a girl around his age, who smoothed her blue-and-white-checked cotton school dress as she rummaged in a box for just the right piece.

"So I see. And who's your friend?"

Relaxing in a comfortable armchair in the corner of the room, Philip ex-plained, "She's Pierre's daughter, Stéphanie."

"Do you have a door?" Nathaniel asked his companion in English.

"*Quoi?*" the girl asked.

Nathaniel rifled through the colorful pile. "This!"

"Ah, *une porte!*"

Just then, a young man approached. In a French clearly honed by years of teachers endlessly drilling verb tenses, he said he came from the Beng village of Totogbé but yearned to emigrate to America.

"Madame," he said, getting right to the point, "can you get me a visa to the U.S.?"

"Well, how's your English?" I asked, surprised by such a direct question.

"*Pas bon,*" he admitted. "But there's nothing here for us. I lost my scholar-ship, the teachers are always on strike, the university is closed for months at a time . . ."

Bertin had told me that less than two months ago, thousands of students had been teargassed while protesting new government austerity measures. Though moved by the young man's frustration, I started to explain the difficulties of living in America without English or family networks. Beyond his dilemma, I fretted that if young men such as this—the urban Beng elite, after all—felt so desperate to leave the country, what conditions would we find in the villages?

≋ "Three more curves to round and we'll see Bongalo," Philip predicted, as if every twist of this pothole-encrusted road remained seared in his memory.

As we neared the clearing in the rain forest that had occupied such an intense period of our lives before becoming parents, my mind turned to our African family. Both our village fathers had died in the eight years since our last visit—Bwadi Kouakou in Asagbé, Wamya Kona in Kosangbé—and so had my friend Lamine, Asagbé's most powerful diviner. I still couldn't quite imagine returning without ever seeing them again.

Philip's mouth looked tight. "At least the car's holding up. So far . . ."

Philip and I remained haunted by the world of trouble our first car had caused us in Africa. A set of flaming crossed wires and innumerable breakdowns had convinced us of the folly of up-country car ownership. But as parents, we now judged these mechanical hassles worth enduring. Though it frightened me to imagine Nathaniel spiking a high fever or being bit by a scorpion, we knew a car could allow us to make a quick escape to the city in case of any emergency.

As Philip turned left onto the narrow dirt road that made the wider dirt road we'd just been bumping down seem like a highway, he called out in a voice trying to sound happy, "Okay, up ahead's our village."

"We're here?" Nathaniel's voice sounded calm enough, though surely he felt anxious.

Savanna replaced forest, and Philip slowed the car as we approached the village. The noise of a car engine's hum attracted young women in bright-colored *pagnes* balancing head loads of firewood and water basins, an old man looking up warily as he hobbled on a homemade cane. Philip inched the car along as our welcoming party enlarged with children who clapped their hands, accompanying our sedan edging carefully along a walking path. A few kids bounded off to spread the news of our arrival—the youngest among them hadn't been born when we last lived in the village. I glanced at wide-eyed Nathaniel, taking in the squat homes made of mud brick, the scattering noisy chickens, the distended bellies of too many young children, but I held back from interrupting his thoughts. He'd need time to process it all.

After slowly snaking our way to the edge of the village, the six small buildings of Amenan's compound appeared before us—including her two-room sleeping house, her mother's small kitchen, and what must be our new two-room house beside a new thatched-roof gathering place, forming a rough circle around the central courtyard. And at the end of the compound, could those two adjoining mud-brick structures with wooden doors be a new open-air bath-house and outhouse?

The courtyard filled with babies, children, grown-ups; at the front of a welcoming party stood my dear friend Amenan, looking just as I remembered her. Balancing a baby tied onto her back—surely not hers?—Amenan's short, compact body announced the same solid hold on life I recalled as her trademark stance; her upturned lips betrayed just the faintest hint of pleasure combined with wistful regret. Philip cut the engine and I hurried out of my seat, eager to hug my old companion. Her restrained embrace reminded me of her royal ancestry as a niece of one of the two Beng kings. Still, her smile widened as she released my shoulders. Our African family surrounded us, and Nathaniel became the object of everyone's attention—this child finally born to the pathetic couple who had seemed in danger of forever remaining childless.

"What a big boy!" Amenan's husband, Kofi, exclaimed in his lilting Ghanaian English as he patted Nathaniel's head. Kofi winked at me. "What is he, ten, eleven years old?"

"Mommy," Nathaniel murmured to me, drawing close, "why does he think I'm eleven? I'm quite sure I don't look eleven. You can tell him I just had my sixth birthday, on April 30th, and I'm only going into first grade next year."

"You can tell him all that yourself, sweetie. You heard, he speaks English."

"But I'm a bit shy."

Kofi chuckled, his two missing front teeth highlighting his easy smile. "Shy? He's just said more than I've said all day. He's a talker, all right. I can see already: this one's more intelligent than both his parents put together." Kofi picked up Nathaniel, whose grin announced his acceptance of this enveloping gesture from a stranger. Maybe this summer would prove a success for our son after all.

Still, I hovered nearby—the glow of Kofi's attention might well fade soon and leave Nathaniel feeling nervous amid all this hubbub. Meanwhile, Philip oversaw the emptying of our trunk as children competed to drag suitcases, boxes, and bags into our new home.

"The beds look great," Philip reported as he came out of the house. Then his voice lowered. "But there are no mattresses, and no other furniture."

"Hmmm, I wonder what happened," I moaned. "I don't think they sell mattresses in M'Bahiakro. We might have to drive all the way back to Bouaké tomorrow. And how are we going to sleep tonight?"

Before Philip could suggest a solution, Amenan's lanky older brother Baa crossed the compound and began the first in a long string of greetings to welcome us back. Then Amenan's daughter Esi asked "*Ka yi mi?*"—Do you want some water? The memory of her birth thirteen years earlier made me blink at the poised teenage girl now standing before me.

"*Wé nan ngo gré?*" asked another of Amenan's brothers—How are the people where you're coming from?

And so, Nathaniel comfortably ensconced in Kofi's welcoming lap and our bags now stowed inside our new house, Philip and I sat on low stools and settled easily into the long round of Beng exchanges.

"*Asé kpa nené wé?*"—How is everything here?—I asked Amenan.

I expected a short, formulaic answer to match the extended welcome finally nearing its close. But, taking my question as an invitation to resume her old role of Consultant on All Things Beng, Amenan loosened her faded wraparound skirt so she could sit on a stool near me. Before we could unpack our suitcases or wash off the road's dust caking our arms and legs, Amenan began to draw from her bottomless well of rumors and chitchat—stories she'd been saving up for me for eight years. Perhaps suspecting I might have forgotten much of my Beng, Amenan began speaking in French. When I responded tentatively in Beng, she switched too, and I strained my way back into the cadences of the language I'd struggled so hard to learn. Old synapses slowly reconnected as I nodded and interjected the obligatory *ah-heh* and *yih* after every few phrases.

Did I remember her cousin Bayo, the flat-chested one with red hair? Amenan asked. Her teenage daughter had learned French and found a job as a nanny in Bouaké. Did I remember her younger sister, M'Akwé? Her sister's son Bapu was now in fourth grade and longed to learn English, and since our last stay in the village, M'Akwé had given birth to twins, but one died in childbirth. Then came Chantal, born after the twins. Almost two-and-a-half now, Chantal was a *yowlé gré*—strong eye—who hit her older siblings and cried a lot. I inserted the obligatory *yih*'s and *Ah, bon*'s to the gossipy narrative.

"I have more to tell you," Amenan said. A woman in the village had fallen mad and was murdered, probably by her husband and four accomplices, all of whom were arrested and imprisoned. Amenan's cousin's son was recently born with a herniated umbilical cord and cried in pain whenever anyone tried to carry him; no one in the village knew any cures for his condition.

I commiserated with Amenan over these sagas, then asked, "And what about you?"

She smiled quietly. "I have five grandchildren now."

Just seven years older than I, and already so many grandchildren? Then I noticed Amenan's mother, Akissi Kro, sitting on a low seat in front of the small building she used as her kitchen. She must have been there all along. The elegant elderly woman sat strangely idle on her stool. From our last stay, I remembered her cooking, chopping wood, washing laundry constantly as she minded the large family's many children. Once she had commented to me, "The only thing that changed after my periods stopped was that I had more energy." Now, ashamed I hadn't noticed Akissi Kro, I rose to greet her in my best Beng.

"*Na ka kwau*"—Mother, good afternoon.

"Mm," Akissi Kro mumbled, then added half-heartedly, "welcome."

"Thank you," I responded on cue.

"How are the people from where you're coming?" she whispered, looking away.

"They say hello," I replied, trying to smile my way into her good graces.

Akissi Kro remained unmoved and to my shock looked off in the distance, abandoning the obligatory greeting sequence.

There was something in her eyes, some deep sadness . . . when we were alone, Amenan would certainly explain whatever ailed her mother.

PHILIP: THE ADVENTURES OF TINTIN

Under a quickly darkening sky we ate our first village dinner at the wooden table that Alma and I had donated to Amenan's compound eight years ago— and that we apparently now had on loan for the remainder of the summer. Nathaniel picked bravely at the meal of rice and dried fish with a thin tomato sauce, and I wondered what must be going on in his head, with the myriad details of this new world bombarding him from all sides: the constant chatter in the competing soundscapes of two unfamiliar languages, Beng and French; the scads of people entering, lingering, and leaving the compound; the unfettered wanderings of sheep, goats, and chickens; the crowds of whispering children that hovered near him, eager to touch his skin, his hair, and yet afraid to do so.

I'd forgotten how fast the sun sinks itself near the equator—soon a few kerosene lamps lit Amenan's compound. I'd also forgotten to unpack our own lantern, which remained buried somewhere among the boxes of gear in our mud-brick house.

"Hey, kiddo, want to help me find that lamp?" I asked Nathaniel, guessing he'd jump at the chance of a break from the circle of curious eyes.

"I know where it is," he said, and I didn't doubt him. My mechanically inclined son had eyed it with interest when we bought it in an Abidjan market, and I'd promised that when the time came I would show him how the thing worked. Nathaniel trailed after me into the house, holding a flashlight, and he lifted the lantern from a box in the corner.

"See?" he said, grinning in triumph.

Back at the table, Nathaniel trained the flashlight as I took the lantern apart, explaining as I went along. "If you pull at this top part here, you can ease out the glass—I think it's called a glass chimney—and then you can get to the wick here at the bottom, and light it with a match."

Nathaniel wore his serious face, nodding as I spoke, as if I were a real authority, an uncommon position for me, since even at six my son had already found his position in the family as the handyman. Back in Illinois, he'd spend hours paging through the pictures of a do-it-yourself home repair manual.

"Okay, but that's not really the bottom. See, if I unscrew the base, you can see it's hollow—that's where we put the kerosene in."

Kerosene. I'd forgotten all about that.

Alma caught my frown and said, "I'll check to see if Amenan can lend us some for tonight." Off she went, and I filled the pause with more patter. "Here, you can see how the end of the wick dangles down into the base. It soaks up the kerosene, so that when we light the wick on top the flame keeps going. That's why we'll have to keep filling up the base with the stuff every week or so. Okay, now why don't you put the pieces back together, to see how it's done. Then you can take them apart again."

Nathaniel set to work with his usual concentration, and Kofi came by with a plastic *bidon* sloshing inside with kerosene. "Ah, look at him, the little man is already in charge."

Half-suppressing a prideful smile, Nathaniel watched as Kofi filled the lantern's basin. I screwed the lid back on, ready to strike a match, but stopped. The wick needed time to absorb the kerosene, otherwise it would burn to a crisp, and that little spectacle would certainly undermine my temporary expertise.

"We'll have to wait a bit," I said to Nathaniel's disappointed face, "the wick is still dry."

Just then Amenan's daughter Esi arrived with a plastic pail steaming with hot water. Something else I'd forgotten: bath time, ritually observed by the Beng each morning and evening. I turned to Alma. "Why don't you go first," I suggested, "while Nathaniel and I wait for that wick to moisten up? He and I can wash later."

"Are you sure?" she asked, but it really wasn't a question. After this long day, pouring cups of hot water over her head from that pail in the new bathhouse would be a welcome treat.

As Alma gathered a towel, soap, and shampoo, Nathaniel gave me a very specific look—half-plaintive, half-insistent—which meant he was ready for some bedtime reading. For the past few months, bedtime reading meant Tintin.

I'd been working my way through the twenty-odd books in the series with him since February, almost immediately after he'd made it clear, with his "Can't we just look into the window of Africa?" comment, that he had no idea what he was in for. I'd searched through the children's section of our local bookstore for something, anything that might prepare him for an Africa much larger than a storefront. Then I came upon a revolving metal rack filled with Tintin books.

I'd never read these books when I was younger, barely knew what they were about, but as I paged through one of the adventures, I felt I might have hit the mother-lode. Tintin was this little Belgian-French fellow, much older than Nathaniel but exuding enough of a childlike air to be in the ballpark for my son to identify with. From what I could see from cover after cover of the books in the series, Tintin traveled from Scotland to Tibet, the Middle East to the Andes, even to the moon.

And inside those covers, what narrow escapes! Tintin—a young journalist adventurer—survived arson and ball lightning, car chases, explosions large and small, poison darts, kidnappings—what wasn't thrown at him from page to page? And through it all Tintin prevailed; nothing seemed to faze his unflappable bravery. This, I'd hoped, might help prepare Nathaniel for his summer in Africa, give him a role model who shrugged off any trouble and kept moving forward. So I bought three in the series—optimistically more than one, but pessimistically not the whole shebang.

Nathaniel loved the books and all the main characters—Tintin and his dog Snowy, Captain Haddock and his creative cursing, the stone-deaf Professor Calculus, and the incompetent gumshoes Thompson and Thompson. As I pointed at the word balloons to let him know where we were on the page, Nathaniel followed the movement from panel to panel with such intensity that I suspected he was teaching himself how to read. We'd go through each book at least three times before he let me continue to the next. Soon enough, though, I grew leery of the colonialist assumptions and dodgy ethnic stereotypes of some of these books, many of them written in the 1930s and '40s. The possible take-away was more complex than I'd imagined, but what could I do, now that Nathaniel was already hooked on these adventures? And so I periodically paused and entertained my six-year-old son with a political critique.

Here we were in the Africa that I'd tried to prepare him for, and still we hadn't finished the Tintin series. With only a few more to go, I had to admit I wanted our reading ritual to linger as much as Nathaniel did. I took out our current adventure, *The Secret of the Unicorn*, and settled into the sloping angle of a palm-rib chair, my son snuggled on my lap with a flashlight, and to the pulse of insect multitudes in the surrounding forest, we began to read.

I'd guessed that there wouldn't be much privacy as I began to read to Nathaniel from where we'd left off (always hard to know where to stop, because in Tintin books, even the cliff-hangers had cliff-hangers), but I wasn't quite prepared for the reaction in the compound. A circle surrounded us—predictably enough—but an incredulous murmur began to rise as well, and I realized that the sight of a father reading a book to his son presented the villagers with an alien tableau. At first I had a hard time concentrating, and my imitation of Snowy's barking—Wooah! Wooah!—only served to draw a larger crowd. I could feel Nathaniel rustle on my lap, unsettled by this curious, noisy audience.

Then André arrived, our host from our first weeks in Bengland, back in 1979. Aside from flecks of gray hair, André looked the same as I remembered him from our last stay, eight years ago. I rose to meet his easy, open grin, and when we finished the ritual greetings, I offered him a chair, then introduced him to Nathaniel, who stood beside me and clutched at my hand. I understood. Tonight, of all nights, he needed me to read to him, and for as long as he liked. I sat back down in that chair, picked up the book, and resumed reading.

I knew this was rude, and what I was doing upset all Beng custom—adults came before children, always and forever. And how could I do this to André, a friend who'd given me one of my first lessons in Beng morality? Our first week living in his compound, I'd been startled by a spider, a huge thing with an alarming leg span until I flattened it. As I flung it away to the edge of the courtyard with a cardboard scoop, André asked if it had bitten me. When I said no, he told me that among the Beng, only insects with "bad characters"—those that bit or stung people—were fair game. "Otherwise," he'd said, in a non-committal voice, "we leave them alone." This short, polite chastening had also been a gentle mentoring, and taught me much about the Beng.

I still felt grateful, but now was not the time for cultural conformity—my son needed me. I continued reading, my eyes trained on the page, unwilling to look up and see what I feared would be André's puzzled, perhaps even reproachful gaze. Yet I knew him to be an attentive father; perhaps he would understand. Soon I heard him whispering in an aggrieved voice to someone in the circle, "What are they doing?"

"Ngo séwé chalo"—They're looking at paper—came a hushed reply, the Beng phrase for reading. And that was that. André settled in for the duration, waiting for me to come to my senses and behave properly.

Meanwhile, Tintin was in a terrible fix, chloroformed and stashed in a wooden crate that two thugs had stowed in a car trunk before driving off to who knows where. Snowy, faithfully chasing the car, soon fell miles behind on the road. I had a difficult time appreciating Tintin's latest dilemma, stuck in the middle of one myself. At the other end of the compound, Alma lingered at her pail bath in the new bathhouse, enjoying her moment of privacy and the warm water in the cool night air, but I really wanted her to come out so she could greet André and get me off the hook. Instead, her happy distant splashing was drowned out by André's silence across from me.

Tintin woke up in some sort of basement reinforced by pillars, and as he searched for an escape route, nearby voices startled him. I paused, having read to the end of the double page. In the past, I'd sometimes peek ahead, say in a sorrowful voice, "And then, that was the end of poor Tintin," and shut the book. "*Daaaad*," Nathaniel would complain, and punch me in the arm. I decided to skip my usual joke tonight. Reading to a child while a visiting adult cooled his heels was scandal enough, but the sight of a child striking his father — however innocently — would more than compound the cultural gulf that was widening moment by moment.

By this time Tintin had fashioned a battering ram to break a hole in the brick wall, just in time to flee from two unsavory and trigger-happy fellows, and now I was deep into sound effects, my "Bang bang! Dong! Boom! Bang bang! Crack!" inspiring many surrounding murmurs. Finally, I heard the wooden door to the bathhouse creak open, and I called out in as cheerful a voice as possible, "Hey, honey, c'mere, André's come to visit us!"

As the slap of Alma's flip-flops drew closer, I turned the page.

≋   I opened my eyes to the dawn's light, stretched out on the hard dirt floor instead of lying on one of the two beautifully crafted bed frames in the second room. We'd spent an unpleasant night on the cold ground, awakened every so often by whatever crawling thing came our way. Later in the morning I'd drive to Bouaké with Kofi, to buy mattresses in the market.

Already, the satisfying thumps of pestles pounding into wooden mortars echoed in the air — our first village morning of many mornings to come. Alma stirred beside me, and Nathaniel stretched awkwardly among the *pagnes* of his makeshift bed on the floor, dreaming who knows what dream, when an unnerving screech shot through the air.

"My god, what's *that*?" Alma said.

"I have no idea," I replied, dragging myself up from the hard floor. I opened our door and looked out at the courtyard and the shocked faces of Amenan's family. On the edge of the compound a rhythmic pulse of unhappiness blared from our car.

Ben's car had an alarm? Why hadn't he told us? I grabbed the keys, ready to put an end to this, and fiddled with the ignition, but starting the car didn't end the noise. I turned the key this way, that way. Maybe all the rattling on the dirt road yesterday had loosened the car-alarm thingy, but just where *was* that thingy?

When I opened the door to get out and poke around the engine, the alarm stopped. Ah, fine, I fixed it, somehow. I shut the door and the siren screamed again. By now the usual curious crowd gathered around the car while Kofi helped me mess around a bit more among the engine's mysteries. Since the Beng believe spirits are behind most confounding troubles, who knew what explanations were already being considered. Truth to tell, I could easily imagine an invisible presence punishing me for last night's breach of Beng social etiquette.

None of my poking about the engine and its hose-like and wire-ish thing-amajigs produced any solution, and I cursed my cozy middle-class American ignorance of basic mechanics. I wasn't going to solve this, and the car alarm would eventually run down the battery. Our only chance was to drive to the closest town, M'Bahiakro, at the other end of those interminable miles of dirt road, where any number of talented mechanics should be happy to take on the challenge.

So Kofi and I were forced to get an early start on our trip to Bouaké. Nathaniel clambered into the car with us—this was too good an adventure to pass up—while Alma stayed behind, eager to begin her first full day of fieldwork in the village. Down we drove, a four-wheel caterwauling headache, and—just like yesterday's trip up to the village—too many of the road's golden memories of years past returned to me: two cracked chassis, three shattered windshields, and more flattened tires than I cared to recount. My main unease with this road, though, came from that time I took a nasty tumble off a bike and the villagers claimed that not only were spirits responsible, but they were still possibly gunning for me. The Beng belief in spirits was so central to their worldview that, whenever I lived among them, at times I couldn't help but feel the tug of it too. I had been, after all, raised as a Catholic, believing in the invisible companionship of my guardian angel.

As we continued to rattle down the road, I found myself able to summon some sympathy for this pampered city car, whose baying might be simply registering shock at the job we were asking it to do for the next few months. "I know, I know," I whispered to the dashboard, with a glance at Kofi to make sure he wasn't listening, "the road here is tough—hey, *life* here is tough. Can't you just suck it up?" But I was also pissed: that damn alarm was screeching out our arrival to any interested spirits who may not have forgotten me. "So you didn't like the road on the drive up yesterday?" I asked, sotto voce. "Well, you're get-ting a bellyful of it now, aren't you?"

I steered us past one intensely curious village after another, each one with a small line gathered by the edge of the road, apparently in anticipation of discovering the source of those mysterious, approaching wails, which turned out to be us. I stared straight ahead, wishing I could invoke invisibility, but in the back seat Nathaniel offered a friendly wave hello. He was clearly enjoying the excitement of this noisy, rattling ride as I avoided holes and rained-out gullies cutting through the dirt road. Remembering Tintin's kidnapping and the car chase from last night's installment of adventure, I realized that this little disaster must have a ring of familiarity for my son, an echo of fictional escapades I'd been reading to him for months. Ah, I thought, as we entered a stretch of road darkened by the thick canopy of trees on either side, *Time and money well spent.*

Kofi remained uncharacteristically quiet as we drove, though I suspected not as a response to the car's wailing. Late last night Alma had whispered to me an extra bit from Amenan's treasure trove of gossip that concerned her husband. Kofi had disappeared to his home country of Ghana for a couple years, leaving no word of his exact whereabouts. He'd only returned recently, and Amenan and the rest of the family hadn't yet forgiven him. Perhaps, staring out the win-dow, he contemplated the unspoken terms of his probation.

By the time we rolled into M'Bahiakro, the car alarm's grating howl was almost an old friend. Kofi rolled down the car window and asked where we could find a mechanic, helpful arms pointed here and there, and eventually we found a sandy corner at the edge of town, with a tin-roofed shack on one side, on the other a towering tree and a pyramid of old tires that climbed halfway up its trunk. A few mechanics worked on cars beneath the shade of the tree while any number of skinny teenage boys—the usual collection of hopeful apprentices—ran errands. Within seconds they surrounded the car. No need to explain why we were there.

With the hood popped open and many eyes more knowledgeable than mine peering into the engine block, I stood back, glad to be relieved of responsibil-ity for fixing this mess, and noticed Nathaniel climbing the pile of tires. This bit of exploring was another benefit of the Tintin books, I thought, once again proud of my parental acumen. His scrambling up—nearly to the top already—looked like such fun that some younger part of me was tempted to follow him.

One of the apprentices tugged on my arm and spoke rapidly in Baulé, a lan-guage I didn't understand. He seemed upset, so I glanced around, a way of asking for translation help, and another young man said, in French, "*Monsieur*, those tires collect rainwater. Snakes can be found there."

Immediately I called out, "Nathaniel, come down from those tires. Now." Though I tried to control the edge of anxiety in my voice, my face felt stiff with fear.

"Why?" he asked, usually a question I encouraged, but not now. If I mentioned snakes, he might freeze at the thought of moving in any direction, so I made up something fast. "Those tires belong to the mechanics," I shouted above the car's alarm, its wail now sounding entirely appropriate, "and they're off-limits, sorry. C'mon down." I walked to the edge of the pyramid, my arms raised, so that after a few steps he'd be able to jump to me.

Any six-year-old understands the concept of coveting possessions, so with a sigh Nathaniel edged down toward me. I kept my arms extended and held my breath, and within seconds he was on the ground, being hugged fiercely for no apparent reason. His face took on a look of lofty indulgence at the inexplicable ways of adults.

Minutes later the head mechanic explained how he was going to disconnect the alarm and did I want this done permanently? Yes, yes, I thought, as far as I was concerned he could take it out and use it to bash in the heads of snakes, keep it, keep the damn thing, I certainly don't ever again want a repeat of this disaster, but all I said was, "*Oui, merci, monsieur.*"

He went to work. I hovered near the car, as if some of the mechanic's expertise might transfer to me by osmosis, but mainly I worried about what I'd wrought by reading so many adventures to my son. The process of Tintin-ification that had taken hold of him was a perfect example of the Law of Unintended Consequences: I'd enlarged Nathaniel's capacity for excitement, but now a certain pulling back seemed to be called for. I watched my son's careful gaze following the mechanic's busy work until the alarm's yowl was finally squelched.

Now, on to Bouaké for those mattresses.

ALMA: THE SPIRIT OF GRANDFATHER DENJU

We heaped spoonfuls of sweetened corn porridge into our bowls. As Nathaniel contemplated this new taste, Amenan came over and announced matter-of-factly, "Aba says he's ready to name *Natanièl*."

At the sound of his Frenchified name, our son put down his spoon and looked up.

"Hey, you're going to get an African name, kiddo," Philip said.

"Do I get to pick it?" he asked.

"Probably not," I laughed. "But they might name you for the day we got here. That was two days ago." I paused. "I think boys born on Wednesday are named Kouakou."

"But I was born on Thursday."

"True—but for the Beng, you were born on the day you arrived in their lives."

"But I wasn't *really* born then, right?"

"Depends on your perspective," I answered, summing up as much Anthro 101 as I judged a six-year-old needed.

Philip and I led Nathaniel to the compound of Amenan's uncle, Aba Kouassi—the chief priest of the village, who had often shared with me his insights into spirits and ancestors. In his courtyard, six stools arranged in a small circle awaited us. Kouassi's grown daughter, my friend Bayo, must have placed them there: now nearly blind, Aba Kouassi could hardly have managed the task.

Aba Kouassi leaned on his cane and walked slowly over to greet us, then indicated our appointed seats. Kouassi adjusted his long cotton robe and, reaching for a bottle of cloudy palm wine on the ground, poured some of the white liquid into a hollowed-out and dried half-gourd. Then he tipped the edge of the gourd to let a few sweet drops dribble onto the dry ground for the ancestors to invisibly lap up, and he downed the remaining contents. Though his blindness slowed him down, he'd performed Beng rituals so many times that he felt his way through the movements without help.

"Grandfathers and grandmothers," Kouassi prayed, "last night, N'zri Denju came to me in a dream. Grandfather Denju said that he's returned to life as this young boy."

He paused to nod in Nathaniel's direction. "So today, we're naming the boy N'zri Denju."

Surely I hadn't understood Kouassi's Beng. But before I could ask Amenan, he refilled the gourd and passed it across the circle to Philip, then continued until we had all made an offering to the ancestors. The ritual drinks concluded, I asked Amenan in French, "Is he talking about the Denju who founded Aba Kouassi's clan?"

She nodded. The weight of my son's new name sank in. "And he founded this section of the village too, right?"

Another nod.

So this was no simple Wednesday or Thursday moniker.

Kouassi added, "Denju was an elder, so your son is an elder, too. For this reason, you must respect him. From now on, you'll have to call him N'zri."

Call my own son Grandfather?

Aba Kouassi continued. "And you must never hit Denju. It would be like hitting our ancestor, Denju. You'd have to wash your mouth out with soap and sacrifice a sheep to the ancestors—especially to the spirit of Grandfather Denju himself."

Nathaniel was always safe when it came to hitting, but treat him as a revered ancestor?

Unaware that a momentous conversation about him was taking place, Nathaniel whispered, "I'm thirsty." I shushed him as Kouassi continued, "Even when you return to your country, you can never hit him. If you do, you'll have to sacrifice a sheep over there. It's serious, hmmm?"

Unsure how to react to our son's new identity, Philip said simply, "Thank you, Aba."

"I'm really thirsty," Nathaniel repeated, but before I could respond, Kouassi motioned Nathaniel over, pulled our child gently onto his lap, and patted his head. "Welcome, N'zri Denju," he murmured.

Grinning mischievously, his daughter Bayo declared, "He's ours now! He'll have to stay here. He can't return to Ameríki!"

"Ah, *bon*?" I inquired, affecting a mock look of worry.

"If you miss him," she chuckled, "you can always come back to Asagbé to visit him."

As we walked back to our compound, Philip explained the morning's ritual to Nathaniel. "So, kiddo, Amenan's uncle said you're an old chief of the village, come back to life."

"Really?" Nathaniel's puckered brows suggested he didn't have a clue what this meant.

"And there's more," Philip added. "We can't ever hit you, and we have to call you N'zri, which means Grandpa."

"What do you think about your name?" I asked.

Nathaniel giggled. "It's great, you can't ever hit me."

"You know we'd never hit you, anyway."

More giggling. "Yes, but now you really can't."

As I squeezed his arm, I wondered how his new village identity would seep in. Already, Nathaniel was reveling in the privileges it would grant him. While I appreciated Aba Kouassi's inclusive dream, I worried about those privileges. Yet how could I argue with our Beng friends' offering? Already, with this naming ceremony, our world and that of the Beng were intertwining in ways I hadn't anticipated.

≋   Though everyone else had turned in for the night, Amenan lingered to straighten up the courtyard, and this rare quiet moment invited Philip and me to approach our friend.

"Big Sister," I started, "there's another reason we've come this summer."

Amenan responded with her signature raised-eyebrow look.

"Whenever we've lived in the villages," Philip continued, "we've always tried to repay everyone's hospitality."

"*Oui, oui*," Amenan nodded, though this wasn't news. Already, we'd begun our usual couple of hours each morning bandaging villagers' cuts and handing out medicines whenever our first-aid training and our well-worn copy of *Where There Is No Doctor* gave us confidence in treatments we could safely dispense.

"But we didn't help everyone that way," I added, "and we'd like to help the whole village this time. We finished the book we were writing about the Beng. We'd like to share the money with the people of Asagbé—and with Kosangbé too, since we lived there first."

Philip joined in. "One thing we've learned in Africa is that in families, everything should be shared." I explained the matching grant the American embassy would offer, and Amenan nodded again.

"*C'est bon*. Did you bring the book?"

Philip went into our house and brought out a copy of *Parallel Worlds*. Amenan stared at the cover photo of a diviner in all white, dancing in a cleared courtyard surrounded by a large audience. She smiled. "Ah, that's Akissi."

Then she leafed through the pages—at first slowly, then more quickly. Her smile faded. "It's written in English?"

I apologized for not having managed to publish a French translation, but before I could wallow in my guilt, Philip joined in. "We're thinking of holding a meeting for the village, and everyone can propose ideas about how to spend the money we're donating."

Amenan frowned. "My cousin Germain's the one who should organize it. You remember Germain?"

I nodded. "Why Germain?"

"He's the *secrétaire* of the village now. He records all the births and deaths. Tomorrow, we'll ask him what to do."

We said good night, and Philip and I retired to whisper new worries.

Since Germain now represented the government's party, he might suggest a partisan project. And could we trust Germain to ensure the money wouldn't get stolen along the way? Ivorians have a great word for this practice:

Bouffer: verb, transitive (1) (slang) to eat

In Côte d'Ivoire, *bouffing* was practically a national sport. Schoolteachers *bouffed* ingredients meant for cooking their students' school lunches, rural nurses *bouffed* medicines to sell on the black market, police *bouffed* bribes from drivers to let them pass a blockade, and—the biggest *bouffe* of all—the president *bouffed* billions of CFAs from the state treasury to build his pet project, the largest cathedral in the world.

In the morning, Amenan sent a child barely older than Nathaniel to fetch Germain. As he entered the compound, I was surprised to see the youngish man I remembered now sporting glasses and a thin and almost-graying moustache.

"Look, here's a book Amwé and Kouadio wrote about us," Amenan said, holding out a copy. Germain picked up the volume, saw it was written in English.

"I can't read it," he complained.

Here we go again, I thought. Then Philip explained that we'd decided to donate the book's profits to the Beng, to be increased by a matching grant from the American embassy. Germain perked up.

"How much money have you made from the book?"

We named the sum, and Germain nodded. "Well, this is good, very good. The government party needs a building in the village. You could pay for that."

"Older Brother," I started slowly, calculating how to decline his suggestion politely. "The American embassy has rules about the projects they'll support, and I don't think they'll accept that one."

"*Bon,*" said Germain, "in that case, you can build new houses for our school teachers in the village. The government is supposed to do that in a few years, but you could do it sooner."

Philip took his turn to run interference. "*Grand Frère,* that's a fine project, but the teachers are all paid good salaries by the government. We'd like to ask the *villagers,* who work so hard, what they would want."

"I'm the representative of the official government party," Germain cut in, "so I can ask people's opinions myself."

Philip and I exchanged glances. Which people would Germain talk to, and who would he *not* talk to? We had anticipated lively discussions about how our funds should be used and had agreed to remain on the sidelines of any decision as much as possible. Now it was no longer a theoretical dilemma.

The boy whimpered and clutched his mother's hand as I wiped away, as softly as I could, the oozing pus from the circular pink sore near his ankle. After I applied antibiotic cream and a bandage, his mother thanked me—"*Ka nuwalé*"—and led her limping child away.

For the past two hours I'd been dispensing pills, cleaning and dressing wounds, my usual morning's work. A score of satisfied patients, however, would change nothing, really, in the serious health needs of this village. At least AIDS hadn't yet come to Bengland; Amenan had told Alma that she knew of only one case, when years ago a young Beng man contracted the disease in Abidjan and returned to the village to die.

I began clearing away our little stash of medical supplies. My efforts were an imperfect endeavor, to be sure, I thought, sighing. Still, everything I did in my life was imperfect, whether crafting a sentence, teaching a class, or trying to love my family well. So why use that as an excuse not to help my friends and neighbors in Asagbé?

Nathaniel, who had hovered beside me for maybe five minutes of horrified fascination at the range of sores and cuts I treated, now sat beside Alma on the other end of the compound, drawing in a sketch pad while she huddled in serious gossip with Amenan.

"N'zri!" I called, "N'zri Denju! How about helping me pump some water?" It was going to take a while getting used to addressing my son as Grandfather.

Nathaniel ran over, as I knew he would, and disappeared into our house, emerging moments later with a large green plastic pail he swung by the handle while clutching to his chest our portable water filter.

"Don't forget the plastic bottles," I said, but Nathaniel was already hurrying back through the doorway. While he collected them, I grabbed the pail and made my way to the huge clay water cistern that the women of Amenan's compound topped off early every morning, thanks to the water pump at the edge of the village. I filled the pail and ambled back to the table, where Nathaniel sat waiting. Poor little guy, I thought, feeling a bit like Tom Sawyer with the paintbrush, because while I disliked this morning task, my son adored it.

"Here, let me start," I said, holding the bicycle pump–like contraption that served as our water filtration unit. Nathaniel had already placed one of the filter's long tubes into the pail, and the second into one of our bottles. Balancing the pump on the table, I pushed up and down on the handle, sucking water from the pail, getting into a good rhythm, and then I said, "Okay, your turn."

Nathaniel grabbed the pump and put his whole body into it, his lips pressed tight, his eyes narrowed in concentration. Earlier this morning Kokora Kouassi had shared another dream with us: the first Denju, the ancestor, was very happy, very pleased with his new namesake. I appreciated Kouassi's visitations, believing that his desire to welcome us had transformed into the details of his dream. Yet Kouassi's gift had also made my son a little strange in my eyes. As I watched him huff and puff at the water pump, I wondered what Nathaniel—N'zri Denju—would make of this new persona the Beng were grafting onto him.

A group of boys and girls had gathered in the compound to watch us, and trying to impress them, Nathaniel leaned in with more effort. He wouldn't last long, but he'd need a way to stop with his honor intact. I waited another minute before suggesting, "Why don't you see if these kids would like to play?"

Normally Nathaniel might hesitate, but he was tired, so he edged away from the table. Two boys about his size held his hands in that casual African way, chanting "Denju, Denju," and, faster than I expected, off they ran, Nathaniel included, all chatter and giggle.

Part of me almost called out, "Hey! Where are you going?" but when I heard hoots and happy shouts behind one of the houses in Amenan's compound, I relaxed. I'd lived long enough in Africa to know that even if he and his new pals ranged farther in the village, they'd never be far from the watchful eyes of some mother, uncle, or grandmother who'd keep them in line. I returned to the task of filtering water.

With five plastic bottles still to fill, I'd be at this for another half-hour. I set our battery-powered tape recorder beside me and slipped in a music tape that would help pass the time. Out popped a shifting mesh of polyrhythms that urged on two huffing accordions and a female singer's smoky-sweet voice.

Bertin had recommended this tape back in Abidjan, and he'd been right on the money. The group, Zagazougou, sounded more like a village ensemble than the fizzy slick African pop that dominated the country's radio, yet this was the music that blared from little market shops and passing buses in the city. Even with the volume knob turned low so I could keep an ear on Nathaniel, within seconds the music had me swaying, a perfect antidote to the mundane rhythm of filtering water.

From the children's background chatter rose a few short bursts of whistling, then more, in a different pattern. I glanced across the compound at Alma, and we both laughed. For the past year or so, there had been days when Nathaniel whistled more than he talked. It was a talent we'd worried about before arriving, since the Beng have a taboo about people whistling in the village—they might be mistaken for spirits, who were thought to communicate to each other by a whistling sound. Amenan had assured Alma that "children don't know anything," so Nathaniel could whistle as much as he'd like. Apparently this remained true even though his identity now included "grandfather."

After a while, the chatter and whistling grew in intensity. Curious about what was erupting behind that mud house, and looking for any excuse to take a break from my filtering duties, I sauntered around the corner and saw the kids scrambling around a pile of old mud bricks, the remains of some abandoned project. Who knew how long those bricks had been there? certainly a short enough time for them to retain some semblance of their original intended function as building material. Nathaniel and his friends had transformed that pile into a more intentional shape: the foundations for what looked like a multiroomed, kid-sized house. Already happily filthy, Nathaniel carved out a linguistic space for himself by augmenting the twists and turns of his whistling with hand gestures. I called Alma over, and we went through our repertoire of Beng praise—"*O geng kpang!*" "*Ka ma dré!*"—for this improvised construction site, while the busy kids barely acknowledged us.

≋   Amenan's husband Kofi and her younger brother Kofi Ba (there were always so many Kofis) huffed through the compound, carrying between them what I first thought was a curious construction of weathered planks until the odd angles finally resolved themselves in my mind as an ancient carpenter's bench.

The two Kofis continued to a clearing behind Amenan's compound, and I followed, along with Nathaniel and the usual flock of curious kids. When they set the bench down at the edge of some coffee trees, Husband Kofi said, "Gideon will arrive soon. Here is a good place to work."

"Thank you, *Nongo*"—older brother—I said, delighted by the news. Alma and I needed a narrow table for our gas-powered cooktop; shelves for books, medicines, and food; a wider table that I could use as a desk for writing; chairs; and a screen door for our house. I'd begun to worry whether we'd find anyone to build them for us. The Ghanaian carpenters who once lived in Asagbé had all moved back to their own country's booming economy. So Kofi had sent word to his friend Gideon, a former carpenter who lived in a village so small it didn't have a name, and who now worked on his father's farm.

These days, even Ivorians moved to neighboring Ghana in search of work, a shocking reversal of Côte d'Ivoire's previous economic flowchart—I'd grown accustomed to thinking of the country as West Africa's powerhouse. Not only had Asagbé's Ghanaian carpenters left, so had the Ghanaian women who worked as prostitutes by night and by day baked and sold soft, lightly sweet rolls the villagers dubbed "Women's Bread." Asagbé had become a village without carpenters, bakers, or prostitutes. I imagined some form of this out-migration must affect every village and town in the country.

Nathaniel quietly circled the carpenter's bench, taking in the peculiarities of this old wreck that had been abandoned by the carpenters. The four legs, boasting their own warped angles, attached to a tabletop made of such gnarled and wavy wood it seemed to undulate before my eyes. I couldn't imagine any carpenter managing a plumb line on this thing. On the other hand, this was Africa, where mechanical miracles were routinely accomplished with the most unlikely of materials, so I withheld judgment.

≋ Gideon arrived that same afternoon, a sack made of tree bark cloth slung from his narrow, bony shoulder. Kofi led us all back to that carpenter's bench in the clearing, children carrying stools and chairs for the adults. Once we'd settled, Kofi assumed the role of speaker for his friend, repeating formally Gideon's greetings and thanks to Alma and me for calling him to Asagbé, that he would do his best work for us, and in turn Kofi repeated for us our thanks to Gideon for his arrival. All through this standard exchange I had to suppress the urge to stare at this young man who looked as thin and frail as anyone I'd ever met. Between his shy smiles, he coughed more than once into his fist.

In Fante and then English, Kofi ticked down the list of the furniture we'd need. I felt pleased to see my friend so at ease in the presence of his fellow coun-tryman. Normally, Kofi struggled with the Beng language as much as I did.

Gideon nodded at each item, and Kofi finally announced, "Nothing is of concern. This chap can do it all."

I suppressed a grin at Kofi's linguistic echo of Ghana's colonial past, and asked, "Even the screen door?"

"Yes, that too."

Gideon took out a stump of a pencil and a tatty notebook and began cal-culating how many planks of wood he'd need, an impressive example of the African combination of skill and low overhead.

As he totted up the numbers, I leaned back in my chair, relieved. I had set my heart on that screen door. Though I would continue spending a lot of time in the courtyard of the compound, giving out medicines and treating minor cuts each morning, enjoying the back-and- forth of Amenan's family during mealtimes, and taking part in the daily surprises that village life offered, a pub-lisher's deadline for a novel loomed large in my mind. While I was grateful that my Beng friends and neighbors—who had no word for privacy in their language—had come to understand that I shouldn't be interrupted when writing because I *wasn't* alone, but instead surrounded by invisible beings asking for their stories to be told, I still needed a space of my own. The Beng lack of privacy extended to their architecture. No village compound was bordered by walls, so anyone could saunter into the busy open courtyard. Walking through a Beng village was like traveling through a series of living rooms. A screen door hinged in front of the wood door to our mud-brick house, however, would allow me to write at a desk inside, while making myself available to the sight of anyone in the courtyard. That way, I wouldn't be suspected of witchcraft. A community-obsessed people, the Beng worried about anyone lurking by day behind closed doors.

When Gideon determined how much wood he would need, Kofi negotiated a price that included his friend's labor and room and board in Asagbé for the length of the job. With everyone in agreement, we went through the stately pace of more ritual speeches and thanks for everyone involved. Already settling in, Gideon pulled from his sack a saw, a hammer, a level and a plane, a broken piece of yardstick and a wood clamp, and set them on the bench.

After a nod of permission from Gideon and an appreciative laugh from Kofi, Nathaniel began poking about the tools. "A Jula trader in the village sells wood, can we go to him now?" Kofi asked.

"You bet," I replied, eager to get the project started. "Hey, N'zri, want to come along and help?"

At first Nathaniel didn't hear me. He balanced the wood clamp in his hands and stared intently into its useful soul.

Casting Spells

JUNE – JULY 1993

ALMA: ANOTHER STORY TO CONFESS

I stood in the doorway of our mud-brick house, sipping the last of my morning's tea and watching Amenan's daughter Tahan, sitting across the compound, line her six-month-old son's eyelids with kohl. Sassandra would look beautiful today. But I suspected that there was much more behind this typical Beng ritual. Though I'd known for years that the Beng believed in reincarnation, I'd never thought deeply about what this meant for the daily lives of infants. Now that I was a mother myself, and my own son was considered a reincarnated ancestor, I had more specific questions to ask besides the everyday issues of who teaches new mothers to breastfeed, how soon after childbirth they return to working in the fields, what they offer as weaning foods. If babies arrived from some other life, how did their mothers and other adults relate to them? I couldn't help laughing quietly at this new direction my research on babies was taking. I'd thought I was leaving the subject of Beng religion behind, but Beng religion seemed to be reclaiming me.

A familiar figure approached the compound, balancing on his head a tray of wares brimming with spools of thread, small candies, and assorted whatnots. My former research assistant, Jean, looked noticeably older: the lean years for the country had carved a few early wrinkles into his forehead.

I hadn't prepared for this moment.

"Hello Amwé," Jean sang out and approached to shake my hand. After we exchanged formal greetings, he said, "When I came to the market, people told me you're here. Welcome!"

Still sorting through my emotions, I asked Jean how he'd been over the past eight years of hard times.

His mouth curled up into that combination of a grimace and a smile that I remembered well. "I've had to sell my radio. My bicycle. I needed the cash."

"How do you get to M'Bahiakro to buy your wares?"

"I walk," he admitted. "I don't have a choice." But Jean's face brightened as he caught sight of our book lying on the table and he read our names on the cover.

"*Félicitations!*"

Forcing my lips into a smile, I tried to match Jean's cheery tone as he leafed through the pages. If he could read English, he'd be appalled. I'd portrayed him harshly in the opening chapters of the very book he was now scanning, with page after page detailing the sudden fits of pique Jean used to display back in 1979 when he would refuse to translate marital disputes or witchcraft accusations; once, he shut down a charming children's dance because he didn't like the insults a few children teasingly threw at each other. Jean had explained that he was sure I'd be interviewed on a Voice of America radio show, and he was determined to paint a portrait of only the pleasant side of Beng village life. With an attitude like this, how could I have fully conducted my research? After too many clashes, I'd had to let Jean go.

"Ah, this is a good opportunity for me to learn a little English," Jean said as he stopped to struggle through a sentence in which he caught his name.

"*Ah-heh*," I muttered, hoping his linguistic talents wouldn't enable him to translate the passage he now regarded.

Months after firing him, I'd discovered that the day we'd moved into the village of Kosangbé, the redoubtable chief San Yao had warned Jean—and everyone else—not to divulge anything of significance to me, otherwise he'd fine them a penalty of no less than an entire cow. It was only in writing *Parallel Worlds* some eight years later that I'd revisited the sting of Jean's early behavior and begun to understand his predicament, and I had found a way in the later chapters to express some sympathy for him—sympathy I never shared with him while in Bengland. I thought with regret of my long-ago outbursts of frustration at Jean, his gentle acceptance of my sudden decision to let him go.

Jean closed the book. "Thank you both, you've done good work."

Jean's expression of gratitude kept me from mentioning that Philip and I had recently been interviewed on Jean's beloved Voice of America, just two days before we'd left for Côte d'Ivoire. It might break his heart to know that the Beng were finally getting the recognition he had long craved, based on research from which I'd long ago excluded him. Or would it?

"It's really good to see you, Jean," I smiled, this time genuinely.

≋ Jostling into our compound, some older boys passed back and forth a scratched and dirty soccer ball in need of air, collecting an audience for a game they wanted to start.

"An'a"—Let's go—said one boy as he grasped Nathaniel's hand, then another boy grasped his other hand, and they led our son away for impending fun. Nathaniel smiled tentatively at all the attention. Philip and I knew the soccer field lay on the other side of the village, much farther than Nathaniel had yet ranged without us, so we decided to follow.

"Jouez, jouez!" a growing group of children called out as we marched to a flat field facing some squat, concrete-block buildings that housed the village's elementary school teachers. Small wooden stools appeared for Philip and me; Nathaniel, too young and shy to play, settled into Philip's lap. As the field filled with the shouts and laughter of the players running back and forth through the dust they kicked up chasing the ball, we strained to follow the action.

"Goal!" the boys next to us shouted.

"Which team scored?" I asked Philip, who answered, "No one's wearing uniforms, so who can tell the teams apart?"

"Then how do they know who's on their team?" our son asked.

"Hmmm," I started, unable to answer this perfectly reasonable question.

"Bonjour."

Philip and I turned to see a young man who had settled silently on the ground beside us without our noticing.

"Bonjour," we responded, surprised that he hadn't greeted us in Beng.

"Bienvenu à notre village," the short young man welcomed us in a French that sounded more village than school.

He shook our hands, and I asked out of habit in Beng, "Ngo mi si paw?"— What's your name? Again he answered in French, "My name is Emmanuel. People call me Matatu, but I don't like that name." His gaze lingered on us a bit too long, his easy familiarity a bit too easy, but then a dusty scuffle on the field diverted our attention.

≋   "Good morning, Little Sister," I said to Au, straining to identify the other faces in her darkened bedroom.

"Good morning, Big Sister," Au half-sang out, shifting a four-day-old baby closer to her breast.

In the corner, I made out an elderly woman twisting dried grasses into string. "Good morning, Grandmother."

"Good morning," she muttered. Why so unhappy? Maybe her knotting work wasn't going well in the dark. On the day a newborn's umbilical stump drops off, the baby's grandmother makes a dried grass necklace, bracelet, and waistband for her grandchild. So this woman must be Au's mother. Perhaps she'd become chattier once she finished her grandson's jewelry.

Au motioned me over to a spot near her. I settled onto a cloth and unpacked my bag of tricks: video camera, still camera, tripod, notebook, pen. Barely a week in the village, and already I was invited to watch and videotape a precious ritual for a newborn. Though laden with gear, I felt light with excitement.

I started scribbling notes. Hadn't Amenan said that aunts also attend this ritual? I couldn't see anyone else. In any case, if the ritual followed Amenan's schedule, the elder in the corner would soon tie three bands around the baby's neck, wrist, and waist, intoning a prayer to her ancestors.

I removed the lens cap from the video camera. Looking through the view-finder, I pointed at baby Kouakou and tried to focus on the small bundle obscured in shadow.

"No, no, no!" shouted the old woman, wagging a finger at me.

"It's fine, Mama," Au intervened. "Let the lady take her pictures."

"I refuse!" the old woman said. "If she takes pictures, I'm leaving."

Flinching at this rejection, I clicked the lens cap back onto the lens and began stuffing the video camera back into its bag. Why had I assumed that Au's invitation meant that anyone else present at the ritual would agree to my video-taping it? I'd never brought a video camera to Bengland before and clearly had to revisit anthropological protocol. My only hope now was to remain as a fly on the wall.

"Don't worry about it, *àh grîh grih ey*," asserted a woman's voice from an-other corner of the room—It's not a big deal.

"What's *she* doing here, anyway?" hissed the grandmother, nodding scorn-fully in my direction.

"I invited her," responded Au. "She's going to record the ceremony. It's good, leave her be."

Au turned to me. "Go ahead, Big Sister, start your camera. Don't mind my mother, she's just old-fashioned."

"Yes, go ahead and start taking pictures," added the other woman. "Don't mind the old lady."

"If you don't want to talk into the camera," Au rebuked her mother in a shockingly firm tone, "then you don't have to. But *we* can still talk to the camera, and the lady can still take the pictures."

From another dark corner of the room, yet another woman's voice joined the dispute. "*You* don't have to talk to the camera if you don't want to," this woman addressed the elder, "but leave the lady alone."

"Well, don't ask *me* any questions," the grandmother warned me.

"Of course, Grandmother," I murmured, amazed at the three young women flouting their elder's authority.

Still, I hesitated as my finger hovered above the Start button: so much for The Triumphant Welcome of the Returning Anthropologist.

Then I did some quick calculations. The old woman was outnumbered at least three-to-one, or maybe the room's shadows concealed even more women. By the standards of democracy, I should go with the majority and keep taping. Besides, I doubted I'd get another invitation to film a first jewelry ritual for a newborn this summer. But the old woman was an elder. In Beng villages, that means a lot. Didn't her opinion count more than any number of opinions of younger women?

We anthropologists pride ourselves for respecting the wishes of the local community—but this tiny Beng "community" of four closely related women was itself sharply divided. I felt stuck in a moral impasse.

"Amwé, aren't you going to take pictures?" Au asked as she held out the baby's tiny wrist to her mother.

I'm probably making the wrong decision, I worried as I removed the lens cap. Another story to confess to my students the next time I'd teach a fieldwork methods class.

≡   His loose-fitting shirt of thick, bleached, home-spun cotton swayed gently as he walked up to us, but the smile on Yacouba's still-boyish face seemed a bit subdued; a wave of guilt claimed me because we hadn't yet managed to visit our best friend from Kosangbé. After we exchanged greetings, I apologized for our rudeness, explaining how packed our first week in Bengland had been, and Yacouba—though with a fleeting grimace—forgave us with his usual grace.

Philip and I had long anticipated the moment when we could introduce our son to Yacouba, and Philip called Nathaniel over from the corner of the compound where he sat balancing a drawing pad on his lap, sketching a Beng-style house. Since arriving in the village, Nathaniel had developed an urge to draw for hours at a time—a way, I guessed, to help him process the Beng barrage of newness.

"Yih! What a beautiful boy!" But Yacouba's deep, enthusiastic voice may have scared Nathaniel, who edged closer to me.

After offering to teach him the African board game of *wali* in which he was a village champion, Yacouba turned to Philip and me. "I'm here on a mission. Come, I want to take you into the savanna. I'll show you some plants I've learned. I've become a healer." Yacouba smiled, barely concealing his pride. "I'm looking for a leaf that can cure a newborn who has a hernia in his umbilical cord."

"I'm coming too," Amenan called out, always eager to gather new knowledge.

I turned to Nathaniel. "Come on, we're going to take a walk with Yacouba."

"Okay." Still overwhelmed by everything, he was happy to stick close to us.

Yacouba led us confidently toward the savanna, and some children caught sight of us and joined our small group. Plucking a leaf from a plant that—to me—looked just like all the plants around it, Yacouba played teacher and asked the growing crowd, "See this one?" Perhaps he was scouting for an apprentice.

"Mmmm?" a boy murmured, looking intently at the leaf's shape.

"It's called *pen pú láná*. You soak the roots or leaves in water and use the water as an enema. It cures dysentery. Want to try it, Amwé?" I laughed. Remembering my horror of all things enema, Yacouba was his old, teasing self.

"This one might be good for N'zri Denju," Yacouba gestured toward a plant. "It's called *propro zó láná*. If Denju ever gets a fever, rub a few of these leaves between your hands with a little water and then wash him four times a day. His fever will go down soon."

I translated the cure to a wide-eyed Nathaniel, who crinkled up his eyebrows. "Will I really have to wash with that?"

Before I could answer, Yacouba displayed a plant that could treat a urinary infection, and another that could cure babies who caught the disease named *gbri*—dirt. He then turned to Philip, some mischief lighting his eyes. "This is a good plant for you, Kouadio. If you get the kind of diarrhea we call *àbibo* that comes with smelly farts"—Yacouba paused to demonstrate the sound effect— "this *trelén* leaf is just what you need."

Nathaniel giggled. Some sentences didn't need translation.

Then Yacouba's voice dropped as he turned to Amenan and me. "The two of you will have to stop walking here, where the savanna meets up with the forest." Yacouba addressed me: "Today's Ba Feh Bey, and women can't go into the forest. But don't worry," Yacouba added, sensing my disappointment, "you can still take pictures when Kouadio and I go into the forest. Just use that camera part that lets you take photos from far away."

"Ah, *bon*?" I smiled at this careful negotiation between Beng religion and modern technology.

≋   Turning to the back seat, I saw Nathaniel staring intently at the wrapped, suffering infant inches away from him. Every once in a while, the newborn's arms started to flail outside the enveloping cloths folded into his mother's lap, then sagged abruptly. He was losing the strength even to produce the startle reflex. Still, every so often, he had the energy to issue a scream that made my jaws clench.

Why hadn't I sat next to Thérèse and her sick child, and put Nathaniel next to Philip? My American values had unthinkingly rated the physical dangers of a six-year-old in a front seat as too risky—without considering the emotional dangers the seemingly safer back seat would expose him to. This seating arrangement begged rethinking, but it was too late. We didn't have a moment to waste now to stop and change places.

This emergency trip to the M'Bahiakro infirmary was far from my day's plan. Earlier that morning, enjoying a Sunday breakfast of a baguette spread with spicy peanut butter, I'd anticipated spending the morning typing field notes from yesterday's visit with a first-time mother and her newborn daughter, when I'd learned that already a passel of female relatives had been chosen as baby carrier, cook, baby bather, and laundress. Then in the afternoon Philip and I intended to drive to Kosangbé for a talk with the feisty elders about our book royalties—a meeting that we'd long dreaded.

My date-book planning had been interrupted by a newborn's sharp wail. I'd looked to the edge of our compound where a young woman approached, the infant in her arms arching its back in pain. People from other compounds appeared and surrounded the mother and child—those shrieks had altered the village soundscape.

"I'm sure it's tetanus," Amenan had said to me. "I've seen cases when I trained in a rural health program with nuns. You never forget." Then she scolded the young mother, "Thérèse, why didn't you bring the baby over sooner?"

"Bandé's only eight days old, he wasn't that sick until today," Thérèse said, shamefaced. A woman who appeared to be her mother added, "I've been trying to find herbal medicines all morning."

Philip consulted our battered copy of *Where There Is No Doctor* and slowly, sadly, read a description of tetanus that matched the infant we saw before us. With only a 50–50 survival chance even with immediate injections of penicillin, we didn't have much time. We convinced a reluctant Thérèse and her mother to bring the child with us to Totogbé, where visiting nurses might help, but once there we discovered the nurses had the wrong kind of penicillin for a newborn. They recommended that we take the two women to M'Bahiakro. Once again the two women deliberated over our offer to drive them to the infirmary.

"There has to be a story behind this," Philip whispered, ever the writer. "I'll bet it's about witchcraft. Are you sure we should go?"

Nathaniel interrupted in a stricken voice, "You're not going to let the baby get sicker, are you?"

"We'll do whatever we can, sweetie," I promised.

On the verge of tears, Nathaniel said, "We *have* to take him. He's so sick."

Finally Thérèse and her mother agreed to our offer, and Philip and I fell into our old role of ambulance drivers on the washboard road to M'Bahiakro. But for whose sake was it this time? Was it to save a baby whose chances of survival were decreasing every minute, or to prove our good intentions to the village at large and forestall any guilt if Bandé died, or to spare further trauma to our own son, who couldn't imagine giving up on a sick baby?

Now, a heavy silence claimed the car's cramped space as we anticipated each new scream. I urged Philip to drive faster. He gripped the wheel and gunned the motor as much as he dared over the road's various traps.

Arrived in M'Bahiakro, we half ran through the eerily empty courtyard of the infirmary and found the doctor in his office, seeing the few patients who could afford to buy the expensive medicines he'd prescribe. He examined Bandé perfunctorily, confirmed the diagnosis, and a nurse enumerated a long list of basic supplies we'd have to buy at the pharmacy across town. When we returned, the nurse attached first the penicillin vial, then a vial of Valium to IV tubes. He hesitated at the sight of several bead bracelets wrapped around both wrists of the shaking infant.

"*Tout ça, c'est quoi, ça?*"—What's all this stuff here?

I sighed. An Ivorian himself, surely the nurse knew that this jewelry was far more than decorative—that the amulets served as magic to ward off spiritual dangers. His question proclaimed his cultural distance from the village, his immersion in All Things Modern.

Thérèse didn't speak French, so I responded, "The bracelets can't harm the baby."

The nurse shrugged and connected the IV. Within minutes, Bandé stopped screaming. At least the Valium had taken effect; it remained to be seen whether the penicillin would too.

Thérèse and her mother decided to stay with relatives in M'Bahiakro for a few days with the baby. We said our goodbyes and walked from the infirmary compound.

"Is the baby going to be all right?" Nathaniel asked.

"Let's hope so," I answered.

"Can't we stay a little while, to make sure?"

"I wish we could, sweetie."

With a rueful shake of his head, Philip said, "We have to get going to Ko-sangbé for that meeting. We can't get in the habit of leaving elders waiting."

I nodded, guessing Philip still felt guilty about making André cool his heels our first evening in Asagbé.

"If we leave now," Philip said, "we should make it to the village on time."

Wordlessly, the three of us climbed into our dust-filled car. This time, I set-tled into the back seat with Nathaniel. As we clicked our seat belts into place, Nathaniel started speaking his fears for the baby, and I chided myself for not having prepared our son for the dire medical emergencies we might well en-counter. Another day, I might have spent this long trip back filling some note-book pages with speculations about why Bandé had come down with tetanus in the first place, or why Thérèse and her mother didn't jump at the two rides we offered them in search of medicine. Instead, I did my best to assure Nathaniel that the doctors would do all they could to save the baby. I hoped the confident note I sounded didn't betray my pessimism.

≋ Yacouba greeted us as we dragged ourselves out of the car, his grin lighten-ing our somber mood.

"Come say hello to my wives," Yacouba invited us. As we walked, few chil-dren ran up to giggle and point at us, few adults greeted us. Kosangbé seemed even tinier, remoter than ever.

We followed our friend to his compound, where he beamed at the small hubbub of life that filled his courtyard. His second wife, Sramatan, stopped pounding rice and his senior wife, Dongi, stood from chopping manioc to greet us. Then the co-wives gathered their too-many-children-to-count around them for introductions. Though the two women, once arch-enemies accused of bewitching each other's babies, had long since reconciled, I couldn't help picturing our friend from many years ago chasing after his two wives as they screamed insults at each other, and ineffectually cracking a whip in the air to get their attention. Their frequently anguished relationship had been set in words in our book, but the passing of years seemed to have brought Yacouba's wives to a new understanding.

The greetings over, Yacouba urged, "Come, let's make our way to the ka-pok tree." As we crossed the village, he gestured toward another compound, where a pretty young woman pounded corn in a mortar while a baby slept on her back.

"Look, do you recognize her?"

The woman resembled uncannily my old friend Mo'kissi, down to her *gbo-*

floto hairstyle of puffy balls named after the sweet doughy treats sold in the market. I strained to recall if Mo'kissi had a younger sister.

"Amwé, it's me." The young woman approached and hugged me, gently taking into account the baby bound to her back.

I blinked. Was this really Mo'kissi, as stunning as ever?

"The baby's my daughter, and here's my son," she said in that soft, calm voice I remembered so well. She gestured proudly to a little boy nearby.

"Congratulations! Look at these two. They're beautiful."

I stared, amazed. In the face of all her suffering I remembered well from our first stay, Mo'kissi seemed to have aged not one day.

Yacouba was eager for us to keep moving, and he gently led us toward the kapok tree. As we continued, I recalled Mo'kissi fleeing the village in disgrace back in 1980. The elders at her divorce trial pronounced that if she wanted to live in Bengland, she'd have to remain with the husband whom she'd been forced to marry—a man she loathed. Mo'kissi had chosen exile. And now, fiercely independent Mo'kissi was back home among the elders who had rejected her. I scarcely knew what to think.

"Why did she return to the village?" I whispered.

"A few years ago, she returned to her husband," Yacouba stated. "They had two children, but then she left him again. She found a Mossi husband, and they had a child together."

"So why did she return?" I repeated.

"You can't stay away too long if your relatives are still in the village." Yacouba paused. "Her mother returned to the village after leaving years ago. So Mo'kissi came back too."

Thus did Beng kin ties claim even the most recalcitrant rebels.

We continued on through the village, attracting a growing cluster of children. Approaching the giant, spirit-filled kapok tree I knew so well, I recalled all the life I'd seen around its huge, flying buttress–style roots: the blood of chicken sacrifices, the tears of funerals, the bitter shouts at trials, and the enchanted yellow weaver birds mystically protected by the chief that nest in its high branches. Now dozens of people waited, assembled under the enormous branches.

I spotted amid the crowd a thinner, more wasted version of Zang, the father of my old friend Nakoyan. Like Mo'kissi, she had rebelled valiantly against an arranged marriage. Unlike Mo'kissi, Nakoyan had given in and became the second wife to a young man in Asagbé, Gaosu—a union steeped in misery. Until recently, Nakoyan had lost all the children she'd had with her husband. Last week in Asagbé I'd met Nakoyan's nine-month-old son who, atypically for a Beng child, clung tight to her, afraid of strangers. Perhaps he sensed his mother's deep parental anxiety.

Zang approached, greeting us in an incomprehensible drunken mumble, then exclaiming over Nathaniel. I winced at the eight-year memory of Zang having drunk the money we'd given him to take one of Nakoyan's dying children to the hospital. Behind Zang lurked another of his daughters, Amlakro, a mentally disturbed young woman who everyone in the village had always considered a snake child—a serpent born into the body of a human. Philip stood between Amlakro and Nathaniel; I guessed he didn't want our son to notice her, didn't want to have to explain a concept that might give Nathaniel nightmares. I was glad when Yacouba led us past Zang and the intense stare of his daughter. Suddenly the chief's compound loomed ahead.

There stood San Yao's familiar figure, hands on hips. His hair had certainly whitened. He had retired as chief of the village, ceding his role to his younger brother San Kofi, and I could see why. The aging Yao's sunken eyes looked haunted—collateral damage, perhaps, from the anxious years when his chiefship had required him to use his powers to fend off any witches that might invade his village.

But his gaze could still cut a diamond.

"So, Kouadio," Yao said quietly. "So, Amwé."

"Father, we've returned to give something to the village," I said.

"Come, let's talk under the kapok tree," San Yao replied.

Gathering his long, white robe around him, San Yao sat on the wooden chair reserved for him. From the crowd, his brother San Kofi approached us and shook our hands warmly.

"My older brother and I welcome you back to the village," Kofi said.

"We're happy to return to our first home," Philip responded, and a long round of greetings followed.

I kept reminding myself to address my remarks to the friendly face of San Kofi rather than his redoubtable older brother. San Kofi had always seemed such a gentle soul—he'd always preferred practicing birdcalls to picking fights. I couldn't imagine him using sorcery to protect the village. Yet maybe his affinity for the birds was his secret weapon. As chief, it was he who now owned those mystical birds that lived in the kapok tree to protect the village . . . and with his knowledge of birdcalls, he could easily communicate with them. Here, perhaps, lay his power.

Finally the time felt right to offer the speech I had hoped to give back in Asagbé—if only Germain had allowed us to hold a large meeting.

I began my rehearsed words in my best Beng. "Our work has gone well back in Ameríki. We've written a book about the villages, and it's made some money."

Yacouba translated my prosaic Beng into the formulaic oratory that the occasion demanded. San Kofi nodded, his expression becoming serious.

"We'd like to share the money with the Beng," Philip added. "After all, this was your work, too."

Serving as our speaker, Yacouba kept restating our workaday Beng, making it more elegant, I hoped. San Kofi nodded and looked at our old neighbor, Ché Kofi, to his left, who said, "The chief says he's happy with your words."

As village chief now, San Kofi wasn't allowed to say any more than the formalities. Ché Kofi must have moved from village joker to chief's speaker.

We explained that we would divide the royalties between Kosangbé and Asagbé, and that a matching grant from our government would double our funds. "The people of Asagbé are thinking about a mill," I said, secretly hoping that saying this aloud might help make it true. San Kofi nodded, then said that he would discuss our proposal with the elders. With that, the elderly men went off to confer in an adjoining courtyard.

PHILIP: ANYTHING BUT INVISIBLE

"Where are they going?" Nathaniel asked.

Stretching out my legs, I chuckled. "To a clearing in the forest, probably to argue for a while." The meeting had gone much better than we'd expected, but now that the elders were off in a huddle, shouting and bitter recriminations couldn't be far behind.

Alma bent over her notebook, writing as much as she could remember of the proceedings so far, and Nathaniel returned to drawing in a sketchbook, his latest passion. The kids of Kosangbé clustered nearby, and Nathaniel kept his head down, concentrating. But I thought he might be showing off, too.

Eventually, Yacouba returned, alone. "The elders are considering a few possibilities," he reported. "I'm not sure the mill will work." Then he left to rejoin the caucus.

This was certainly unusual, sending a messenger to communicate clearly with us about their deliberations. And so far, still no shouting.

Yacouba reappeared. "They're still considering different ideas," he announced and then vanished again.

Again, we heard no hint of arguing. "Hmmm, they must be up to something," I said, but Alma only laughed at me.

Finally, the full group reassembled under the kapok tree.

"We've discussed many ideas," Ché Kofi began. "We don't want the mill that Asagbé is considering. We're afraid it would cause too many fights. Instead, we'd like to fix our water pump. Our women struggle every morning to get water out of our old pump. The young girls can't manage at all."

Some elderly women nearby nodded their heads vigorously. Ché Kofi continued, "One of Asagbé's pumps works with a foot pedal. The women there say it's much easier, and it gives more water. We've heard we can replace the hand pedal on our pump with that kind of foot pedal. That's what we'd like to do."

I sat back on my chair beneath the kapok tree, proud of the male elders for placing the interests of the village women first on their list, especially considering what I'd long considered to be Beng men's indifference to the burdensome workloads of women, from the daily gathering of wood and water to the constant triple demands of farming, cooking, and child care.

I turned to Alma and whispered, "Can you believe it?"

"It seems too good to be true," she said, her eyes glistening a little. "Don't you think the embassy will be happy to fund this?"

"Absolutely. Let's agree quickly, before the elders change their minds."

If Alma and I had any foolish illusions that we'd managed to capture in writing the fluid Beng world, it was clear from this meeting that we'd never be able to pin these people to the pages of a book. After years of writing and revising, our village friends and neighbors had quietly, slowly, become characters to us, actors in a parallel literary world. Yet after all our writing, how little we knew them. Here were gathered our former crusty neighbors, so effortlessly—and differently—themselves. Once so divided from each other, now they appeared just as easily civil, and surprisingly united in their judgments. The normally cunning and often dictatorial chief, San Yao, had searched with his younger brother for consensus, and the usually sharp-tongued Ché Kofi represented the elders gently yet eloquently. These two men had changed, matured in the years since we'd first met them.

Or had Alma and I merely underestimated these aspects of their personalities, not given them enough weight in our portrayals? Oh, the curse of a writer, endlessly revising. Clearly, the last page of our memoir was not our last page with the Beng.

≋ I looked up from the table, and there was that fellow we'd met at the soccer game, the odd one. He stood too close to me, smiling, but I'd grown used to my sense of personal space being violated—the Beng standard of curiosity allowed close quarters.

I went through the usual exchange of morning greetings and prepared to return to my typewriter when he backed away a few steps and brought something he held in his hand up to his face, positioning it. It looked like one of those Marlboro cigarette hard packs. Avoiding Beng once again, he said, "Bonjour," made a clicking voice, moved a foot to his left, and clicked his tongue again.

The cigarette pack, I guessed, was his idea of a camera, and when he clicked again I decided to go along with the joke. I sat up straight and drained my face of all humor or expression—the typical stiff pose any Beng person assumes in front of a camera. Two could play at this game of cultural reversal.

A few people in the compound laughed at the sight of me. The fellow—I couldn't remember his name—took this as encouragement and again and again took imaginary pictures of me until the joke lost its energy, became strained. I returned to my noisy typing, the keys' clacking competing with his clicking sounds, which he now directed toward Alma and Nathaniel. Soon enough, he gave up the game—but then pulled up a chair and sat beside me. I tried to pretend he wasn't there, but he held out his cigarette pack for me to admire, and I gave it a glance. It had been altered somehow, and when he saw my interest, he smiled and motioned for me to hold it.

He'd cut out a circular hole near the top of both sides and used the excised cardboard to fashion the raised rim of a lens. He'd even rigged up a little square in one corner as a viewfinder. Clearly, his little joke was more premeditated that I'd imagined.

"It's my camera," he said in French, "and me, I'm the prime minister."

I nodded, admired his prized creation, gave him a nod of respect, and then showed the cigarette pack to Alma, then to Nathaniel. Our son carefully examined its intricacies, then raised it and took a picture of the young man, who feigned unhappiness that the fiction of cultural reversal had been broken. He demanded his camera back and soon left the compound.

"Wow, what a comedian," I said to Alma, though I couldn't help wondering if there was something more to this encounter; his unhappiness at the end had seemed a little too real.

It wouldn't take long for us to find out, since Amenan was already making a beeline to us, her juicy-gossip face firmly in place—at times like this, Amenan was most Amenan.

She found a seat, smoothed a few crinkles on the *pagne* skirt over her legs, and said, "That was Matatu. He's mad, you know."

"Mad?" Alma repeated, unsure she'd heard correctly.

"He used to be the village barber. He's been well for over a year, but since you arrived in Asagbé . . ." Amenan paused. "Now he's back to saying that he's the prime minister of Côte d'Ivoire."

Alma glanced at me, her face stricken. What I thought had been a performance of village stand-up now slipped from the realm of entertainment onto another stage, one on which there was little laughter. Anthropologists like to think they can be invisible while conducting fieldwork, even if they know that's impossible. Now, our simple presence might actually be triggering a young man's return to mental illness.

Or was our presence here really all that "simple"? In this village with no electricity or running water, we'd brought with us a caravan of Western goodies — examples of a world far beyond the reach of the villagers. Just on the table before me sat my typewriter, our water-filter hand pump, and Alma's tape recorder. Our material entourage was anything but invisible.

≋   The following evening, as we scarfed down bowls of rice with bits of smoked fish and tomato sauce cooked for Amenan's family by her daughter Evelyne, Matatu returned to the compound. After the usual call and response of Beng ritual greetings, following local etiquette we invited him to join us for dinner, but he shook his head. Over his shoulder was slung a large sack that he set down beside us, taking out an offering of oranges and pineapples.

It was a generous gift, and we thanked him. Matatu smiled and announced, "I really worked hard this morning!"

Three flashlights on our table caught Matatu's eye, and he picked them up one by one, admiring their various details. "*C'est joli, c'est intéréssant*," he repeated, with the air of a connoisseur. He flipped knowingly through an abridged edition of *Robinson Crusoe* I'd been reading to Nathaniel at bedtime, then stared intently at Alma's watch. In a spirit of exchange, he produced a weathered rectangle of a card for us to examine, from the Centre de Santé Mentale in Bouaké, which recorded his name and diagnosis: *manifestation psychose*.

Was this an admission of his madness, or did he not know what it said?

Cautiously following Matatu's lead, I said, "*C'est intéréssant, c'est joli*," and he nodded his head solemnly, accepting my appraisal. Then, as if some test had been passed, he dug deeper into his sack and pulled out what he presented as valuables — an empty match box, a brown zipper, two empty perfume bottles — while saying almost pleadingly, "*Ce n'est pas bon?*"

"*Oui, c'est très bon*," Alma and I replied, a call-and-response exchange we continued as Matatu took out of his bag in succession a cassette without a case, an old leather wallet, an empty medicine bottle, a crumple of tin foil, and a discarded wrapper from a pack of cookies we'd given Nathaniel as a treat. Matatu must have found this last treasure by scrounging through the garbage at the edge of the compound. Alma and I exchanged careful glances.

Then, seemingly out of nowhere, Matatu announced, "In Abidjan, I'll drink ice water!" Before Alma and I could fashion a polite response, he reached into his bag again and drew out a tin of sardines. He pried open the can and demanded a plate from Amenan, saying, "I am the prime minister of Asagbé." After emptying the oily fish on the plate, he ate with his fingers, gorging himself in a kind of miming, I imagined, of Big Man behavior. Between bites, he declared, "I have a car made of gold" and "Tomorrow I'm going to buy a bicycle and give it to my father." Alma, Nathaniel, and I sat as if pinned to our chairs, watching in fascination, and I fought the impulse to cover my son's eyes, afraid I might call attention to the disturbing edge of Matatu's strange performance.

By then a crowd had gathered—a common village reaction to any diverting behavior. Someone said something to Matatu in a derisive voice. He stopping licking his fingers and responded with a shout in French, "You're a bad guy, I'm going to throw you in prison!"

Everyone laughed; I grimaced inside at the crowd's casual cruelty. Matatu pretended not to hear, but in short order he collected his bag of tricks and left.

As the crowd dispersed, Bertin, who'd been watching from a corner of the compound, walked over and said in a whisper, "It's witchcraft that made Matatu mad." I offered a noncommittal "Hmmm," though I secretly agreed. The witchcraft, however, was not the village variety; instead, it had the pedigree of Western culture, and Alma, Nathaniel, and I appeared to be its inadvertent practitioners. Like it or not, we were casting spells.

≋ Kofi and I knelt before the hinged frame of what would soon become a screen door and we stretched mosquito netting around the edges, pressing thumbtacks into the wood to hold the mesh in place. Amenan scooted away the kids who snuck in too closely. "*Ngo drewolo!*"—They're working!—she repeated as they scattered. I kept my head down but couldn't blame them for wanting some of the action, since it looked like so much fun. The moment she turned her back, they drew closer, Nathaniel included.

Throughout the past week, he had snatched every chance to watch Gideon mark measurements with the stub of a pencil; or smooth the uneven edges of the boards with his plane, leaving their tan curls of wood in its wake; or hammer in nails with precise taps. I'd often sit beside Nathaniel and watch too, though mainly I enjoyed my son's fascination.

Now I turned to Nathaniel, standing at the edge of the crowd of kids, and asked, "Hey, N'zri, want to give this a try?" In a blink he knelt beside me, while Kofi chuckled—everything about my son seemed to make my friend laugh.

I held the netting tight while Nathaniel pressed tack after tack into the frame, its soft wood easy for him to manage. When we finished, Gideon set about attaching the frame's hinges to the doorway, and Kofi and I returned to the workspace behind the compound to fetch my new desk.

By the time we returned, Gideon was testing the screen door, swinging it nicely back and forth, and then he held it open as Kofi and I carried the desk inside. We placed it in the first room, where I'd be in full view of any curious soul.

Gideon returned to his open-air workshop, ready to tackle the chairs and shelves, Kofi headed off to check his traps in the forest, and eventually Nathaniel and his buddies left to repair the walls of their building project, which the goats of the village had once again climbed and destroyed overnight. On the other side of the compound, Alma and Amenan still schmoozed about who knows what sort of gossip. I'd hear the juicy details later. Now, I was alone.

Alone.

This was a compromise I could live with—a small measure of privacy for me, and a sufficient lack of privacy for the comfort level of my village neighbors, since anyone could just peek in. The mesh of the screen door was perfect—allowing a breeze in while keeping flies and mosquitoes out.

I set about organizing and within a few minutes stood back to regard my little makeshift office: neat piles of paper in one corner, typewriter smack dab in the middle of the desk. What appeared strange and modern to the villagers seemed like a museum piece to me, after ten years working on a computer. Knowing there'd be no electric outlet within twenty miles, I'd dusted off the typewriter that had served me so well in two previous trips to Bengland. At the airport when we arrived in Abidjan, my black typewriter case was an object of curiosity for more than a few people on the customs line. I might as well have been carrying a daguerreotype box camera from the nineteenth century.

"Excuse me, is that a . . . typewriter?" a woman standing in line behind me had asked.

"Uh-huh," I'd replied, the tone of her voice making me defensive. A few moments of silence passed, and then she said, "Excuse me again, but I can't help asking—why do you have a typewriter?"

"Well, I'll be living in a small village up-country for a few months. No electricity."

"Ah," she'd said, as if she finally had me pegged, though I doubted it. Most likely she assumed I was some sort of missionary, off to save lost souls in the rain forest. I'd kept my mouth shut—why contradict a stranger, and who cared what she thought anyway?

Now I sat down, took out a piece of paper, listened to the roller's familiar rasp (how many thousands upon thousands of times had I done this in the distant past?) as I wound the sheet into place. Though I had a book review to finish for the *Chicago Tribune*, of the novelist John Hawkes' alternative version of *Black Beauty*, the cruelties of horse breeding seemed a universe away. So I turned to my novel, which felt right at home. Why shouldn't it, since it was secretly influenced by nearly fifteen years of travel back and forth to Africa? The mother in the novel poured her repressed self into characters that she invented and acted out before her children, and this felt to me like something the Beng might describe as spirit possession. Her oldest son Michael's alertness to her transformations molded him into seeing beneath the surface of the world, creating a kind of permanent, personal culture shock. Though not a word or hint of Africa appeared in any corner of this suburban American setting, Africa was the invisible essential air my characters breathed.

I began to work into a scene of a family outing to a bowling alley, where the mother sees the balls lined up on the racks as haunted faces, those three finger holes like hollow eyes and an open mouth silently screaming. I could feel the family's tension, but I didn't quite know what to do with it. At moments like this, I was happy to be working on a typewriter. Though its keyboard may have been a callous builder for fingertips (press, press, press, PRESS), and the simplest sentence on the page was birthed in a clatter, and any mistake required gooping a coating of white paste over the error and then waiting for it to dry, the machine's limitations did force me to slow and think longer before committing words to the page. This was a machine that offered a built-in antidote to a novel's necessity of ever moving forward, forward.

I typed a little, thought more, then typed a little less, until I heard the screen door swing open. There stood little six-year-old grandfather Nathaniel, sketch pad in hand. Since we had arrived in Africa, he'd developed an interest in art that he had never shown before, and now he drew pictures of the village and portraits of his young friends that were startlingly accomplished, as if combining an anthropologist's gaze with a child's clarity.

I was about to ask him to show me his latest drawings when he said, in a professional tone, "Don't let me disturb you," and pulled a chair alongside me. Suppressing a smile, I tapped a bit at the typewriter for his benefit as he drew, and tried not to move.

Faster than I would have imagined, he finished. Without a word he passed the sheet of paper to me, and I couldn't believe how clearly he'd captured the mechanical niceties of the typewriter, the wrinkles of concentration on my brow, my beard, even the fly that rested on the screen window behind me.

"This is terrific," I said to his instant smile, but before I could continue, voices out in the compound cried out "Denju, Denju," and my son ran from the room to join them.

ALMA: TOO EXPENSIVE TO DIE

"The baby's back," Amenan said softly as I looked up from typing field notes.

"Which baby?" I asked, then understood. "Ah, that's great! So the medicine worked?"

"No," Amenan shook her head. "The nurse told Thérèse to take Bandé back to the village. He might not last another day."

"But . . ."

"If he died in M'Bahiakro, it would be very expensive. There'd be fees for the cemetery, for the casket, for the death certificate from the mayor's office, for the gravediggers." Amenan paused. "It's much cheaper to die in the village."

After all our efforts and hopes, now this. A dying baby. What would I tell Nathaniel?

"It's not your fault, Amwé."

"If only she'd come to us sooner . . ." I already knew that Thérèse's family had used an old razor blade to cut the umbilical cord, for the simple lack of a few CFAs a new one would have cost.

"You know, Thérèse's father is my cousin," Amenan said, and so—perhaps to distract us both from our sadness—my friend fell into her role of Anthropologist's Assistant. "Thérèse was forced to marry a man she didn't like, in an arranged marriage," Amenan began.

"I should've guessed," I mumbled, shaking my head.

"She had a daughter with him," Amenan said, "but she also kept seeing her old lover. The guy got hold of a shirt of her husband's. He took it to some sorcerer, a *mauvais type* who used it to curse her husband."

"Ihhh?"

"The husband heard about the curse and got scared. He divorced Thérèse and fled the village."

I nodded. There was a lot more to this story than I had imagined.

"But Thérèse grew tired of her lover. She took another and became pregnant by him—but he soon left her. While she was pregnant, she took a new lover.

This man refused to marry Thérèse, but he agreed to recognize her baby as his, once it was born—even though he's not the real father."

I grabbed my notebook and started madly charting these ruptured relations, my genealogy featuring the slash marks of divorce.

"After the birth—ten days ago—Cei Nicolas, Thérèse's father, went against the lover's wishes and named his new grandson, using his own last name."

"Was that so bad?" I asked. "After all, Thérèse isn't married to the guy."

"Well, in Nicolas' view, the baby had no legal father," Amenan explained. "But there's a new national law against a baby taking a grandfather's last name."

Now I understood why Thérèse's family had been reluctant to accept help for this child, conceived as he was in the turmoil of rejection and curses. Then came that most taboo of thoughts: maybe we shouldn't have expended so much effort to "save" the baby. Philip had immediately sensed that something was wrong, but I'd ignored his hint, listened instead to our son's pleas, convinced we needed to make every effort we could—even if the baby was doomed.

Later that evening, Amenan and I forced ourselves to visit Thérèse's compound and offer our condolences, while Philip stayed behind to console Nathaniel. The dying newborn lay on his back, covered head to toe in cloths, as for a corpse. My friend caught me by surprise when she whispered to me grimly, "It's as if he's already dead. One could say he is dead . . ."

≋ Walking to the edge of the village, I caught sight of Bertin and Augustin sitting across from each other at their worktable, bent over my jumbo-sized pink notebooks. They looked rather prim and proper in the pressed city slacks and shirts they insisted on wearing every day, while doing their best to ignore the teenage girls giggling around them. I suppressed a smile. Even with these flirtatious distractions, my research assistants were making excellent progress transcribing the interview tapes I kept adding to their work pile.

"How's it going today?" I asked.

Bertin frowned.

"IPA problems?" When I'd trained them to write out my taped conversations using the International Phonetic Alphabet to accommodate the ŋg's and aw's that marked the Beng language, I'd worried that this new alphabet might prove tricky at first.

"No, it's not that," Augustin started. "We're both just working on babies' babbling today."

I'd discovered that adults and older children often trained newborns to participate in conversations by asking them questions in Beng and then waiting for a response in the form of a gurgle or other random noise. Teaching infants the rhythm of conversation was a high priority for the Beng, and transcribing these exchanges could provide persuasive—and charming—data.

"The problem is," Bertin complained, "people come over to see what we're doing and they try to grab our headphones to listen to the tapes. Sometimes it's hard to get our work done . . ."

"Hmmm," I started, glancing at the girls behind them who kept giggling and whispering.

"Some people get mad at us," Augustin added, "when we don't let them listen to the headphones."

On previous visits to Bengland I'd transcribed my interview tapes myself, late at night and behind locked doors to keep them private. But I'd planned for assistants this summer to transcribe my tapes, and since this would be during the daytime, they'd have to work outside, otherwise they'd arouse suspicions of witchcraft—yet with the utter lack of privacy anywhere in the village, I'd worried about sensitive information becoming grist for the gossip mill. Besides, no one would confide anything if they thought I couldn't be trusted to keep our conversations private. So I was relieved when a colleague back in Illinois had mentioned a tape recorder whose playback function only operated with headphones—this would prevent anyone from listening in. But now, those headphones seemed to be causing their own problems.

A middle-aged woman carrying an infant sauntered over, curious about the growing crowd.

"What are you doing?" she asked.

"We're writing down some babies' words," Bertin explained.

"Yih?" the woman exclaimed. "Let me hear." With that, the woman reached for the headphones perched on Augustin's head.

"No, it's for our work," he objected.

"You're just transcribing some babble now, right?" I asked.

"Yes," Bertin laughed, "it's not really words at all . . ."

I made a quick judgment. "Well, I think it's okay if you let her listen."

The woman crinkled up her nose in confusion at the first sounds, then understanding crossed her face. "*O jowalo, deh*"—The baby's talking, all right!—she laughed, then passed the headphones to one of the flirtatious girls, who passed it on to another, then another, and the group erupted in gales of laughter.

One of the girls, grinning, turned to the baby on the woman's back. "Here, you listen," she said, adjusting the headphone to fit around the small head. His eyes widened when recorded babbling filled his ears.

The girls clapped their hands in excitement, and their noisy hilarity encouraged the baby to respond with his own babababa's.

"This could solve your problem," I told Bertin and Augustin. "Whenever someone wants to hear what's on the headphones, let them listen to a baby babble tape. There's nothing sensitive there, and people will love it."

If only every fieldwork dilemma could be so easily resolved, I thought with relief as I presented my assistants with yet another new tape to transcribe.

PHILIP: THE WAITING FAX

Asagbé's weekly market blossomed color in the center of the village's usual shades of brown and gray. Here fruits and vegetables spread over mats on the ground, brightly patterned *pagne* cloth and ready-to-wear dresses hung from the wooden beams of impromptu stalls, and women sat before their cooking pots of treats—corn porridge; *attiéké*, a couscous-like grain topped with spicy fried fish; packets of roasted peanuts; lightly fried dough balls rolled in sugar. Traders from around the region flocked once a week to this portable shopping mall that traveled from village to village.

What caught Nathaniel's eye was a busy corner where Jula mechanics repaired bicycles: tightening chains, repairing or replacing tires, balancing wheels, replacing lost or twisted spokes. Nathaniel parked himself as close as he could to the action, and aside from a few chuckles, no one seemed fazed by the little boy who sat beside them, taking in their techniques, inspecting their tools, indulging in his endless fascination with all things mechanical. Once, at a highway rest stop back in Illinois, I'd paused while my then four-year-old son bent down and peered up at the bottom of a huge truck. Finally satisfied, Nathaniel continued walking with me, and before I could ask what he'd been doing, he said, as much to himself as to me, "I always wanted to know how an axle worked."

Two of Nathaniel's new friends, Bapu and Meda, joined us and sat beside him, quietly keeping company with his curiosity. Bapu, at age eleven barely taller than Nathaniel, was his family's great hope to continue from primary school on to middle school. Meda, at eight, looked much smaller than my son. The two Beng boys were wiry but healthy little kids by local standards, though clearly their bodies hadn't been nourished in the same way as this American boy beside them.

I could see that Nathaniel had settled himself before these mechanics for the long haul. "N'zri Denju," I said, "I'm going to help Mom buy food. When you're done watching, come back to the compound with Bapu and Meda for lunch, okay?"

He nodded, and I set off, but first I wandered over to Jean's small corner of the market. He stood before a square wooden tray divided into small compartments holding small candies, combs, nail polish, boxes of matches, cigarettes he'd sell individually, his inventory mostly small indulgences in an economy that these days could spare precious little extra cash. At the end of the day he'd simply balance the tray on his head and walk a few miles back to his home in Bongalo.

Jean and I greeted each other, and I bought enough candies to give out in Amenan's compound, some nail polish for her daughter Evelyne who cooked for the family this summer, an extra box of matches, and cigarettes for Kofi, but only a few. Amenan still kept her husband on a tight rein, and would disapprove if I gave him the gift of an entire pack. Kofi's latest absence from the family wasn't his first disappearing act, apparently, and I wondered if Amenan suspected her husband might have a second family back in Ghana.

Jean thanked me a little too profusely for my small purchases, and I worried how often he ate in a day. Just as with the villagers of Kosangbé, the reality of Jean standing before me supplanted the portrait Alma and I had fashioned for him in our book, one that could have managed an extra drop or two of sympathy. Yet this Jean before me surely wasn't the definitive Jean either, any more than the Philip he was selling these matches and candies to was the final me.

As I left in search of Alma, I wondered if there might be something we could do to help Jean, a way to try to right a wrong that—being unable to read English—he didn't even know we'd committed.

≋ Alma and I returned to Amenan's compound loaded down with a sack of rice, a half dozen dried fish, and a basket of fresh vegetables—our contribution to her family's larder for the week. Not long after, Nathaniel returned to the compound with Bapu and Meda. Heading straight for our mud-brick house, he emerged with his plastic bag of Legos.

It was hard to imagine him surviving more than a week without those blocks, which served as the developing architecture of his thoughts as he constructed houses and castles, every manner of building or vehicle. We'd worried, though, that in the usual crush of kids in the compound the various pieces would get scattered and lost, or there might be a mad grab for the shiny plastic blocks and they'd quickly get divvied up. Play is largely communal in the village, and the sense of private ownership of a toy is a privilege most African children can't begin to imagine. We'd warned Nathaniel about this, told him children in the village might want to share his blocks more than he was used to, so at first he'd kept his Lego playing behind closed doors late at night, just before bed.

Bringing out his Legos to share with Bapu and Meda was a sign of friendship and trust. Nathaniel spread his blocks across the surface of the wooden table, and a noisy cluster of kids soon surrounded the three boys. But no one touched anything; instead they stared at his hands adding block to block, slowly making something recognizable out of disparate pieces—a little car. Then, without prompting from his hovering parents, he offered it to Meda.

≋ So far, the day had gone smoothly.

Barbara Brown had been driven up from the American embassy in Abidjan to visit the village, and the Asagbé elders had decked out the concrete pavilion that served as a political meeting place with a lush floral arrangement. Alma and I suspected Germain was using the occasion to siphon some prestige from the visiting guest, but Barbara also served as a reminder that someone above had final word about how the royalty and grant money would be spent: a nicely balanced stalemate.

Alma gave a brief speech to the elders introducing Barbara, and her slow, halting delivery surprised me. I was usually in awe of my wife's language skills, the way she could chat in Beng with her women friends, but the formality of this occasion made her choose her words carefully. Then Barbara spoke in French and Germain translated, taking a lot longer with his own words than she had with hers. Again I suspected that he was spinning the event to his advantage.

Though the meeting ended with the elders still undecided about a project to propose, Barbara was presented with the gift of a live chicken. She held it upside down by its bound legs, gave a flustered thanks, and the driver from the embassy relieved her of the restless creature. He set it in the trunk of the large black sedan. Now was the time to head off for a similar meeting in Kosangbé, where everything had—against all odds—already been decided, and where I guessed there was another chicken in Barbara's future.

Alma and Nathaniel sat beside Barbara in the back seat, but before I could settle up front with the driver, Matatu appeared lurching through the crowd, and he opened the car door. Barbara's expression of curiosity switched to alarm when he declared, holding the handle of the open door, "*Moi, je suis le premier ministre.*"

She pulled the door shut, and the car began to slowly ease away. Matatu stared wildly at the car, as if preparing to chase after it. I didn't want to think of the scene if anyone was forced to restrain him, so I had to think quickly in my poor French.

"*Monsieur le Premier Ministre, ce n'est pas possible,*" I began, which allowed him to pause and calm down. "Madame feels ashamed before you, because you're such a powerful man—the prime minister! She doesn't deserve to drive in the same car with you."

This made no sense, but my mollifying tone seemed to satisfy him for the moment. Before he could reconsider my shaky logic, I sprinted to the car and off we went.

"Who was that?" Barbara asked, and as Alma explained I turned to look through the rear window. Matatu stood in the middle of the dirt road, the very image of an abandoned soul, staring after us. There was a good chance our escape would not be the end of this story.

≋ In the darkness of almost dawn the alarm bleeped—too loudly—and I groaned in bed as Alma turned off the racket. Within minutes the three of us were dressed, our bags already packed from last night, and we hurried to haul our gear into the car for a trip to Abidjan. Though this was impossibly early for us, the hard-working women in our compound had already risen, some preparing a fire for the morning meal, some marching off—with empty basins balanced on their heads—to gather water at the village pump.

We wouldn't wait for breakfast. Amenan frowned, probably hurt that our hasty departure reflected poorly on her role as our hostess. But we wanted to leave before Matatu woke, to avoid a scene if he caught wind of our plan and insisted, in that strange imperious way he could slip into, on coming with us. The village's Prime Minister had been sulking for days about being left behind when we drove with Barbara Brown to Kosangbé.

So now we bade Amenan goodbye and hopped in the car. Driving along the edge of the village toward the main road, I hoped that the echoing, resonant *clunks* of the village women pounding cornmeal in wooden pestles would disguise our car engine's puttering, all the while keeping a lookout for a young man who might be chasing behind us.

Once clear of the village, Alma and I relaxed and settled into the idea of a little R & R. During her visit, Barbara had invited us to an American embassy–sponsored Fourth of July party, and we'd immediately accepted. While in the city we could also stock up on medicines for the villagers, call our families back home, and fatten up Nathaniel, who wasn't adapting well to Beng cuisine.

Arrived in Abidjan, we checked into a hotel, washed off the dust of the trip, and set out first to a pharmacy for medical supplies, then to a bookstore near the Cocody *marché*, which offered a reliable selection of English-language books. We'd been reading at a steady clip through a stack we'd brought from the States for Nathaniel, and who knew when we'd return to Abidjan? Time to add to that stack.

From the teeny selection of children's books in English, I chose a thin volume of Greek myths, which might put in context for Nathaniel some of the local spirit possession and witchcraft stories he'd already gotten wind of in the village.

Alma searched through the children's selections in French, and then she held up a familiar-looking book and asked, "Do you have this Tintin—"

"That's not a Tintin book," I said, peering closer, "it's—let me see that."

Another adventure series by Hergé? *La Vallée des Cobras*. The cover featured what seemed to be a brother-and-sister team named Jo and Zette, and inside, the same cliff-hanging adventures. But these were French editions, rough going for my limited language skills. Perhaps if I took the illustrations as cues, I could make it up as I went along.

"Why don't *you* read these to Nathaniel?" I asked, handing the book to Alma.

"Honey, come here," she said, beaming, and while they huddled by the shelf, I glanced over another table's spread and noticed a two-volume encyclopedia in French, probably designed for middle school students, the text accompanied by plenty of color illustrations, photos, and charts.

This might be a perfect gift for Jean. He'd done well in school when he was young, and his father's refusal to support his further studies was the tragedy of his life. I could see him plunging into these books, even if they offered only a taste of the education he'd always wanted.

"Hey, look what I found."

≋ While we sat at a white-clothed table beneath dimmed lights and waited to order, I looked across at Nathaniel, skinnier than usual. Though he had already begun accumulating his first Beng words, and had settled gleefully into the village children's responsibility of chasing the compound's chickens to bundle them into their coops for the night, he found West African food too spicy. He didn't care for the pasty balls of cooked yam *foutou*, or the gooiness of okra, and last week he'd lost interest forever in a savory monkey stew at the sight of a tiny paw floating among the chunks of meat. Rice he'd eat, doused in soy sauce just like he preferred at home, and this was why we'd come to a Vietnamese restaurant that, I guessed, was run by former refugees from either the war with the French in the 1950s, or the Americans in the 1960s.

Alma and I felt the painful irony of our son's losing weight because he didn't care for village food, while too many children in that same village sported distended bellies, malnourished because there wasn't enough to eat. Yet we had to feed our son, help him stay as healthy as possible in case illness struck—malaria, dysentery, or any number of other maladies common among the Beng. So here we sat in an Abidjan restaurant, about to enjoy a meal that was beyond the imagination of most villagers.

Our white-suited waiter was a Mossi man whose ritual facial scars—long incised lines—ran down both sides of his deeply dark face, from temple to jaw line. A taciturn man, he conducted business without a word, giving up only a nod, a glance, or a lifted eyebrow.

We ordered crispy shrimp chips for starters, which Nathaniel munched on happily, and then he dug into a small bowl of rice, but when Alma tried to interest him in a green vegetable whose name we didn't know, our son wore his stubborn face, a flag to the world that He Would Not Be Moved. A direct approach was doomed, but there might be another way to establish the principle that trying new food is good.

"Too bad," I said, my sigh exaggerated just enough to catch his attention, "because you'll never get a reward from the Food Fairy."

Nathaniel's eyes searched my face for a joke, or a trap, but I was prepared. "You never heard of the Food Fairy? She's like the Tooth Fairy, except that she gives children money when they try a new food."

Before the question could cross his mind, I said, "She's an African fairy. You're lucky that you're here this summer."

Alma's lips pressed together. She wasn't going to let herself laugh, or even smile, but the struggle was clear on her face, and if Nathaniel saw her, all would be lost.

"How much?" he asked.

"You mean, how much money?"

He nodded, but I could see this wasn't a question necessarily fueled by greed; instead my son was testing the perimeters of the tale, a sign that he teetered on the edge of belief.

"100 CFAs," I made up on the spot. "That's about 25 cents. Four of those will get you a dollar."

"How much do I have to eat?"

I almost had him. "Just one whole piece of something new. Just to see if you like it. If you like it, you can eat more. If you don't, you don't have to."

"How do you get the money?"

I guessed he was thinking of the traditional tooth under the pillow—another sign he was circling the hook.

"It just appears, like magic." I'd figure out that detail later.

Before Nathaniel could consider this too closely, Alma had already forked a carrot cut in the shape of a flower—its odd shape qualifying it as a new food. "Want to start with this?"

While Nathaniel ate, I slipped my hand in my pocket, searching by touch for a 100 CFA coin, very carefully, so as not to let the coins jingle. How many did I have? Alma kept up a patter, asking Nathaniel if he liked it, why or why not, his face turned to her as they talked up the relative merits of the dainty morsel of a petalled carrot. I glanced over my shoulder, on the lookout for our waiter, afraid his stoic face might break into disapproval at the sight of me bribing my child to eat, but he stood with his back to us at the other end of the dining room. I snuck my arm along the side of our table and slipped the coin on the tablecloth beside Nathaniel's plate.

"So, good?" I asked, as if I hadn't been listening.

He made a face. "Not very."

"But you tried it, and that's what's most important. The whole thing, and not just a bite?"

"He ate it all," Alma said.

"Then the Food Fairy should pay up. Maybe she has already."

Nathaniel searched the table with a skeptical air, his belief hanging in the balance. Then his eye caught the glint of something nearby hidden beneath the lip of his plate.

He lifted the coin, and Alma gushed, "She came, the Food Fairy came!"

Nathaniel held the coin in his open palm, contemplating its magic with an air of stunned acceptance. Any Beng diviner would have been proud.

"It's yours, buddy," I said. "Better put it in your pocket."

"Now," Alma said, already poking a fork among three or four oddly shaped mushrooms mingled in a sauce, "what else is new for you to try?"

≋   Climbing the stairs to the second floor of the American Cultural Center, a book review in hand to fax to the *Chicago Tribune*, I thought of how strange it had been to read, while living in an African village, John Hawkes' twisted take on raising horses. Once I sent that review off, I'd call home to my parents, try to give them an inkling of the summer's complexities so far.

Instead, a fax waited for me. Marie Josiane Ogou, one of my friends at the center who I'd met during the Ivorian writers conference three years ago, handed me a sheet of paper, her eyes so stricken that I hesitated before reading it.

My father had died two days ago, on the Fourth of July. The news had taken this long to reach me because the center had been closed those days for the holiday. Before I could allow myself to react, I thought of us that day at the embassy party, where the general American expatriate community had enjoyed a hotel's swimming pools, water slides, and a well-stocked snack bar. Children ran about squealing with glee, and though Nathaniel wasn't much of a swimmer, he knew fun when he saw it, and glommed onto the smaller water slide. My father must have died back home during that holiday party.

Alma joined me, gasped at the fax, began cooing sympathy that I couldn't quite hear, and soon I was being settled in a room by the staff, where I could spend some time alone. The desks, the window's view of palm trees, all seemed alien.

For months, I hadn't allowed myself to consider the possibility of my father dying, because I had so much left to say. The last time I saw him, we'd sat together on a couch in the North Carolina condominium he'd moved to from New York, for a retirement filled unexpectedly with too many visits to doctors and hospitals. In less than a month I'd leave for Africa. In another room my mother sat by herself, atypically content in her dementia, watching television shows that she felt certain were about her childhood, as if the years before she met my father had somehow come to life.

We'd only be gone for the summer, I'd certainly see him again, I told myself. So I fought the impulse to speak as if for the last time. I said we'd be back soon, then grew alarmed as I veered into an awkward little speech about my affection for him and the warmth of his humor—words that held a hint of finality. There was more I might have said, less kind words that I pushed back down inside me. Instead I kissed him on the forehead and said goodbye.

Alma entered the room. "I think I've found a flight that might get you back in time for the funeral. If we're lucky, there's a good chance I think, when you get to the U.S., that you might make a connection to . . ."

"Let me think about this, okay, hon?" I murmured.

"There's not much time if . . ." she began, but then kissed me lightly, squeezed my arm, and left me to myself again.

My father had always been proud of my travels—something he'd never been able to do himself, because of my mother's agoraphobia. He'd read the manuscript of *Parallel Worlds* with pleasure, filling in the blanks from the letters I'd written from Bengland over the years that had kept out such minor details as bouts of malaria and close encounters with poisonous snakes. And now here I was, so far from home I might miss his funeral.

I heard a light knocking on the door. Time is passing, my wife's tapping tried to tell me. Alma had surely worked out the best possible plane route, and while I doubted it would get me home in time for the funeral—I'd heard that in her voice when she first explained the schedule—at least I'd arrive soon after.

Outside the window, the swaying palm trees, the whoosh of passing traffic brought me back to Abidjan and the tropical heat outside this air-conditioned room. I paused. If there was one final gift I could give my father, it could be a trip he had never taken while alive. Instead of returning home, I'd return to the village and give him a funeral there, a Beng funeral, a posthumous adventure. After having read my letters and memoir, he had come to know many of the people who would attend his funeral in Asagbé—more so than at his funeral in North Carolina, where he was a newcomer. Maybe this was self-deception, but I thought he would have loved the idea.

Things of the Heart

JULY – AUGUST 1993

ALMA: MAD TO BE MODERN

5

Philip inched our car into Amenan's compound and a children's circle of laughter, shouts, and song greeted our late afternoon return to the village.

"What are they saying?" asked Nathaniel.

"They're welcoming us back to the village."

Philip braked, and a jumble of eager hands opened the door and yanked Nathaniel's arms as he unbuckled his seat belt. Suddenly our son was hoisted in the air and carried about the compound by his playful friends. His cautious temperament fades daily, I thought, as Nathaniel waved and smiled at us. We hauled out our luggage, and Amenan approached to welcome us.

"Big Sister," I started, in Beng, "when we were in Abidjan, we heard news that wasn't sweet."

"Eh?" she responded, her eyes suddenly concerned.

"We received a message that Kouadio's father has died back in Ameríki."

"Auuuuuuu, *a kunlia*," Amenan immediately intoned in a high-pitched wail.

Distracted in his grief—he'd remained unnervingly silent most of the six-hour drive up from Abidjan—Philip managed to mutter the obligatory *maa* to Amenan's offer of condolence.

"It was too late for Kouadio to fly home for the funeral," I explained, "so he'd like to make a funeral for his father here, in Asagbé. Would that be possible?"

Amenan said, "I'll go talk to Aba Kouassi."

Minutes later, Amenan's uncle crossed his compound to ours. Through the dark of his blindness, he walked carefully, balancing a half-gourd in his hand: there must be water in it.

"Older Brother, he's here," Amenan said softly to Philip, who nodded and managed a wan smile. Though back in Abidjan he'd called his family and explained the decision to honor his father in the village, I worried that he was wracked with regret.

Aba Kouassi addressed Philip. "Kouadio, they told me the news. My condolences."

Thankfully, this formulaic exchange didn't require my doleful husband to contribute much to the conversation. "*Maa*," he barely whispered.

"We'll offer this to the ancestors," Kouassi continued, and he tipped the edge of the gourd, spilling a few drops of water onto the ground. Then he started praying to my father-in-law's spirit.

When he finished, the appearance of a line of mourners surprised us, their keening wails delivered on cue: "*Weeey! Weeey! Weeey!*" The funeral had already begun. As I knew from years of attending Beng funerals, over the next week or so there would inevitably follow a more formal line of mourners, a somber gathering in Amenan's compound, an all-night singing session or two, and an animal sacrifice to the spirit of the departed. The Beng were experts on mourning; now we would experience the round of rituals from a more intimate perspective.

≋ The next morning, the air still chilly from an overnight rain, Amenan stepped among the puddles in the compound to sit beside Philip and me and fill us in on village doings. I wasn't surprised to hear her begin with a story about Matatu. Shortly after we'd left the village, he came to our compound, and when Amenan explained that we'd gone to Abidjan, Matatu announced that he'd follow us. Soon he picked a fight with his older brother over borrowing a bicycle. "His brother refused to lend it. Who rides a bicycle all the way to Abidjan? But Matatu grew so angry he attacked his brother with a machete."

I sucked in my breath. Matatu's madness had moved undeniably from eccentric to dangerous. After the failed assault, Amenan continued, Matatu fled and wandered around the Beng region. When a group of farmers heard he was nearby, they abandoned their fields and beat a quick path back to their village, terrified that Matatu might try to attack them too. They sent messengers to Asagbé, begging for strong men to bring him home.

"Once Matatu was returned to his compound," Amenan said, "his older brother strapped him to a big log. That's where he's been for the past few days."

Amenan paused to let the weight of her words sink in, then added, "But Matatu is trying to free himself. He's pulled so much that his hand tied to the log has swelled up. They'll probably free him even though he's still crazy . . ."

"My god, this is terrible!" I burst out.

Philip said nothing, but I read misery on his face and imagined he was thinking that our presence had fueled Matatu's deepening madness. He, too, deserved riches . . . and why not? But what else might come of Matatu's longing?

≋   Breakfast over, Philip and I sat side by side in front of our house in Amenan's compound; soon villagers would be dropping by, asking for whatever small medical help we could provide. Across from us, Nathaniel huddled in a corner of the compound with his friends Bapu and Meda, whittling sticks of soft wood into what appeared to be slingshots. Now that the school year was over, Bapu's mother had been sending him to the fields to scare away hungry birds from the growing corn; maybe Nathaniel and Meda were helping Bapu construct an arsenal for his new responsibilities. I'd have to go investigate soon, notebook in hand.

For now, though, Philip and I discussed the matter of which sheep to choose for a sacrifice in honor of his father. Kokora Kouassi had told Amenan that this part of the funeral ritual must be conducted soon.

"About 3,500 CFAs is the going price," I reminded Philip.

"Yeah, but the sheep they brought by yesterday looked a little scrawny. I'd like to take a look at a couple more before—"

A young woman arrived in our compound, a small child bundled in her arms; an elderly woman who was surely her mother walked slowly alongside her.

After the exchange of ritual greetings, the young woman told me her name was Au Ba, and she pointed at her child. "He's sick," she said simply, "he just won't eat. Do you have any medicine?"

Pounding corn nearby, Amenan looked up, eyebrows raised. Philip and I checked the child for fever, sores, pains: nothing obvious stood out. Still, something unsettled me about the boy. His face looked more mature than his tiny body. I asked Au Ba his age.

"He's a little more than two years old."

Sighing, I retrieved the measuring strip that lay tucked away in a box in our bedroom, offering an easy way to confirm malnutrition. Wrapped around the wrist, the paper bracelet displayed notches that, in a healthy child, should correspond to each month of the first three years—a yardstick of health or misery.

"My god, look at this," I whispered to Philip as I rolled the marked strip around the boy's wrist, leaving plenty of paper dangling as overlap. "He's in the red section"—*Severely malnourished*.

I remembered another way to assess malnutrition—maybe this one would provide happier results.

"Little Sister, can I peek into his mouth?" I asked Au Ba.

"Yes," she said.

I counted only four teeth on top and four on bottom—half the number he ought to have at his age.

Amenan stopped her pounding and approached me. She knew the mother and quickly explained the boy's story. "He was healthy his first year." Then Au Ba's mother joined in. "When he's healthy, he eats. When he gets sick, he barely touches food."

"But if he sees any meat, he begs for it," Au Ba added.

Philip and I conferred. "Little Sister," I started, "we don't have any medicines for him. Right now, we think he just needs food. Why don't you come every morning, and I'll give him something to eat?"

I offered Au Ba a can of sardines. Arching her eyebrows in skepticism— she'd clearly hoped for a quick fix of medicine, not food—she nevertheless accepted the can and agreed to return the next morning.

"Let's take his picture," I added, hoping this would encourage her to return. "Then we'll take another at the end of the summer and see how much he's grown."

To jump-start my nutritional therapy, I offered the child a cookie. He took a listless bite, then spat it out. He seemed almost indifferent to life.

Au Ba put her child down from her lap and adjusted her *pagne*, preparing to leave the compound. But the boy's legs were so thin and weak he could barely stand. After a few steps on the path, Au Ba lifted her son and carried him.

≋ Some elders had recently taken a perilous journey to discover why many clan members had fallen sick lately. Traveling to the afterlife, they hoped to meet up with their ancestors. After one unsuccessful trip, the elders returned and finally encountered some ancestors who pronounced that back in the land of the living, people were falling ill because a sacred treasure owned by the Beng king had been stolen a few years back. The thief took the treasure to Abidjan, where a white person bought it—and immediately died. But apparently the punishment meted out by the powerful object did not make up for the desecration: Beng people continued to fall sick.

So Amenan had told me. As I typed notes on these miraculous occurrences, dozens of questions arose. How did the elders reach the afterlife, and how did they return alive? Which elders went on the mystical journey, and could I talk to them about their otherworldly experiences? Who had betrayed the Beng people by selling the sacred treasure, and what happened to the traitor? Did the white buyer in Abidjan have any idea about what he had purchased?

I sighed. Tracking down the intricacies of this amazing tale was a tempting project, but I still had so much to pursue in my research on Beng infants. This was always the downside of fieldwork for me—too many intriguing paths to follow.

I looked up from my typewriter to see Yacouba enter the compound with five young men who I recognized from Kosangbé. The delegation—natty in their pressed pants and shirts—oozed a certain energy that suggested exciting news. Philip joined the greeting party, and Yacouba served as *gan klé lali*—the speaker who talked for the group.

Philip and I had recently sent word to Kosangbé that, after obtaining estimates for the water pump conversion that the villagers had requested, we calculated that we had enough of our own funds left for another project. I wondered if this small delegation had arrived with a proposal.

"We're here to thank you for yesterday," Yacouba announced, opening the session in classic Beng ceremonial style. "The elders of Kosangbé are very grateful for the help you've offered the women of the village."

"*Maa*," Philip said on cue, while I offered the woman's response, "*aung*."

"Since you'll have some money left after fixing our water pump, the elders have considered many options and have decided they would like something for themselves."

"Ah, *bon*?" I asked.

"Yes, our village needs chairs."

"Really?" Philip asked, his writer's curiosity piqued.

"*Oui*, it's not for the elders themselves but for their guests," Yacouba explained. "Whenever we host a wedding or funeral or a big meeting, Kosangbé is shamed. After visiting elders have walked two or three kilometers, they're tired, but we can't offer them comfortable chairs like the ones that Asagbé and Bongalo have."

I pictured the brightly colored plastic chairs I knew well from those villages. They looked garish to me, but perhaps the normally conservative elders found comfort not only in the chairs' molded seats but the appearance of modernity.

"We're the most important village, ritually," Yacouba proclaimed, "so it's especially terrible . . ."

"Mm-hmm," I nodded in sympathy.

Yacouba lowered his voice. "We tried to raise the money ourselves, as the other villages have done, but we're too poor."

Philip whispered to me, "What a fabulous idea. I say we go for it. How expensive could the chairs be?"

"I have no idea," I answered. "And I don't know where to buy them. But we might have some adventures finding out."

Philip turned to Yacouba. "Bon. We'll see if there's enough money for the chairs."

"Thank you Kouadio, thank you Amwé," Yacouba said in Beng, and as his companions rose to shake our hands, Yacouba remembered an afterthought. "And the elders say they don't care what color the chairs are."

PHILIP: MY FATHER'S AFRICAN AFTERLIFE

Darkness had long fallen when Amenan's older brother Baa arrived in the courtyard, guitar at his side and accompanied by a group of friends, to sing some of his songs in honor of my father's death.

Neighbors strolled in slowly, followed by villagers from compounds farther away, far more than I'd expected. When an old person dies, Beng funerals celebrate a long life lived, and my father's seventy-five years seemed to qualify him. So the crowd had come out of respect, but I guessed that people were also drawn by the promise of Baa's performance. I had recently asked Amenan why the usual village evening dances hadn't been performed since we'd arrived in the village. "We dance when we're happy," she'd said, adding, "these days no one is happy"—words that revealed yet another cost of the country's continuing economic troubles. Well, I thought now, at least my father's funeral would offer the village some temporary pleasure—Baa's jaunty music was popular, and not all the songs tonight would be sad.

As the crowd grew, Amenan and her daughters brought out extra wooden stools, chairs, and straw mats from the compound's various buildings. Then she left for a few minutes and returned, carrying a liter of the heady homemade brew called kutuku that she must have bought from a neighbor, to pass around among her guests—another good reason for a large turnout. Yacouba entered the compound, and I rose to greet him, so grateful he'd biked all the way from Kosangbé for this ceremony, grateful for the support of his embrace as he said with real feeling the Beng phrase of condolence, "A kunlia." I nodded to André when he arrived—thankfully, he had forgiven my rudeness from that first evening of our return to the village.

Kokora Kouassi sat on a stool facing the guests, a gourd holding water in one hand, a shot glass holding kutuku in the other. Amenan turned to us and said, "Aba is about to pray and invoke the spirits."

His head bent to the earth, Kouassi began to speak:

Dear Grandfather Denju, spirit of our ancestors,
Here is water for you,
Take it and drink

Kouassi paused, then tipped first the gourd, then the shot glass, dripping water and the clear alcohol onto the earth.

Father of Kouadio, you who are dead,
Here is water for you,
Take it and drink

Again, Kouassi made his offerings, then set the gourd and glass on the ground before continuing.

Father of Kouadio, your son is among us
To share with us your funeral rites

He doesn't forget you,
He will never forget you

Rest calmly, the earth
Will be soft for you

Give good fortune to your son,
His wife and child

The nearly full moon glowed softly, casting night shadows over our growing circle. Tall and lanky, Baa stepped forward with a calm demeanor I admired because it was the opposite of my usual noisy internal traffic. Baa strummed his guitar, his friends clanged iron bells quietly, rhythmically, and as music filled the cool night air, I huddled with the comfort of my wife and young son in the middle of the compound and listened to the lilt of the songs. Baa sang too quickly for me to make out individual words, but Amenan, sitting beside us, whispered quick translations.

Our only father, he's gone, he's died,
He has been snatched from our hands,

Look: my only father, who fed me, is dead,
Snatched from my hands

I stirred uncomfortably in my chair at these words. If only the grief they embodied could be so simple. My father had worked hard all his life, each day framed by a grueling commute to and from New York City. As a child, I don't think I'd ever appreciated the sacrifices he made to offer his family a middle-class life. Yet once home, he began drinking before dinner, and by nine o'clock he could barely recognize anyone. Perhaps that had been his intention. My parents' marriage had long ago become a misery, punctuated by my mother's frightening bouts of rage. When I grew older, she turned that anger on me, and the habit of my father's long-suffering ways made it impossible for him to step in. Was my leaving for Africa this summer my way of paying my father back for his inability to defend me? I squirmed in shame.

Baa sang again, a humorous song about a young woman who argued with everyone. Glad the evening had finally begun to offer lighter moments, I continued to nurse my glass of *kutuku*. Then Amenan began murmuring the lyrics to another song:

As long as you're not dead yet,
Problems will always follow you.
Problems will always follow us in this world,
Even if you have money,
As long as you're not dead yet,
Problems will always follow you
In this world of people

The time had come for me to give a speech, and I stood, cleared my throat with a cough, and in halting French said that my father had worked hard all his life, loved his family, and knew of many of the villagers there tonight from the letters I had written to him from Bengland, and that he would be happy that they had come tonight to the ceremony. As Amenan translated, I felt more and more the fraud for pretending all had been well between my father and me, and I couldn't have felt more relief when Baa and his friends started another song.

Before I'd left for Africa this summer, my father had complained about a sentence in *Parallel Worlds* that mentioned "my unhappily married parents." Though now I wished I had apologized for causing him pain, at the time I'd said, "But it's true, so why be so upset?"

"Because now everyone will know," he replied simply, disappointment palpable in his voice. My father had struggled with the necessity of my writing the truth as I saw it, especially when the emotional details of my short stories cut a little too close to home. Tonight I felt his reply the way a Beng person might hear a parent's curse, as the sort of words that might make someone go mad.

Across from me in Amenan's compound, Yacouba nodded his head to the music, and I remembered that of course the Beng mask their own dramas through ritual. Yacouba's father had died since our last visit to Bengland. I could only imagine my friend's conflicted feelings during what must have been an animist religious funeral, since Yacouba had converted to Islam as a way to reject his father, whose drunken wanderings through the village had shamed him.

Nathaniel had collapsed into sleep on the mat beside us, and he looked so peaceful, eyes shut, mouth half-open. I wondered if we should wake him so he could take in this latest phase of an African funeral for his grandfather. No, there would be more ritual moments in the days to follow, let him get his rest now, since he'd spend tomorrow playing hard with his friends under a harsh summer's sun. Baa continued his singing, Amenan continued translating his verses about backbiting friends, a wife's erratic behavior, but I no longer followed closely, lost in words of accusation, apology, even of comfort, that I'd never again be able to say to my father.

≋ I pounded at the typewriter keyboard, its slow clatter the soundtrack of my novel, when through the screen door I heard Germain's voice offer his greetings in the compound, followed by Alma and Amenan's responses. I decided to stay put in the imagined setting of a model train museum, where a secret hid among a tableau of tiny plastic figures in a miniature downtown.

"Kouadio?"

Alma peered inside. "Germain is here, with Matatu's father, Yao. You might want to be part of this."

I did. Here was another drama I felt bound to, however unwillingly. I left my desk and sat beside Alma on one of the chairs set out in a circle.

With typical Beng formality, Germain began to speak for Matatu's father, asking us to go to Bouaké to buy medicine for his son's madness. Alma and I had grown accustomed to Germain trying to squeeze some financial or political advantage out of any situation, though in this case he clearly employed his position in the village to represent Matatu's family in their crisis.

I turned to Alma. "What do you think?"

She kept her voice low, even though we were speaking in English. "I don't think drugs are the answer . . ."

"I agree, they didn't help him the first time. And anyway, after we leave, those pills or whatever would run out."

"Maybe an African solution would be better," Alma said, and she turned to Amenan. "Aren't there good healers among the Jimini," Alma asked, now in French, "ones who can cure madness?"

Amenan nodded, pleased that the discussion had turned to an area of her expertise. "I know a Ghanaian man who healed a woman in Asagbé. She used to be mad, but he cured her. He's very good. He lives nearby, in a little village, Kaklagbé. It's between Wati and Bedara."

Alma and I looked at each other. Since we felt certain that Matatu's illness was deeply embedded in his own culture, maybe this was worth a try, at least for starters. We offered to pay for the healer's treatment. Matatu's father and Germain huddled into their own whispering, then announced that the family would have to decide.

Their decision wasn't long in coming. Matatu soon broke free of his hand chains, though he no longer seemed violent. I would drive with Kofi to Kaklagbé, where my friend would ask the healer to take on the case.

≋ Kokora Kouassi had arrived early in our compound to make a pronouncement, and he sat across from us, his nearly blind eyes staring into the distance, the morning air chilly from last night's rain.

"Welcome, Aba," we greeted him.

Speaking through Amenan, Kouassi began, "Kouadio, I had a dream last night." I nodded. "Your father appeared to me. From *wurugbé*."

From *wurugbé*, the Beng afterlife. I didn't know how to respond. It never occurred to me that my father, after his Beng funeral, would become a member of the culture's afterlife. In *wurugbé* the dead are also supposed to understand every language, and I could only shake my head at the idea of my father now speaking Beng easily, considering my years of struggle to learn it.

Noting my silence, Kouassi added, "In the dream, he and your son met."

"Ehhh?" I said, slipping into the Beng style of encouraging a speaker to continue.

Kouassi then recited what Amenan said was a Beng proverb, before translating: "You need two hands working together to wash the back."

I glanced at Alma, but the slight frown across her otherwise amazed face—and what did my face look like?—told me she didn't have a clue either. She returned to scribbling furiously away in her notebook while I waited, guessing that what followed would clear up the mystery.

"In my dream," Kouassi continued, "your son told his grandfather that he had come to visit us with his mother and father, and that he had been named for N'zri Denju." Kouassi paused, stared in my direction. "Your father agrees with our ancestor N'zri Denju that this new name for your son is all right."

The original Denju then appeared in Kouassi's dream as well and introduced himself to my father as the ancestor that Nathaniel was named for. Kouassi said, "Your father and Denju are both proud of your son."

I shared that pride, though it left me a bit dizzy: my father and Nathaniel and I were now united within the nurturing dreams of my old friend Kokora Kouassi. As I listened, I felt multiplied into mourning son, doting father, and respectful "grandson" all at once. But Kouassi wasn't finished.

"Kouadio, in my dream your father asked for a favor. He's new at death. He misses human food. He'd like you to leave an offering outside your doorstep tonight. He just wants a taste, to remember."

I assured Kouassi that I would do this, though I wasn't certain what to offer. I said, "Aba, my father doesn't know Beng food, it's different from what he ate in America."

He smiled. "He'll like it," adding that the original N'zri Denju, apparently, would be joining my father for this snack. Kouassi suggested that we collect four empty cans of tomato paste, fill two with palm wine and the other two with bits of cooked yam. This was just the sort of meal, unfortunately, my father would have enjoyed when alive, his diet always low on vegetables and high on starches and alcohol. It might very well have contributed to his cancer. Yet what harm could it do him now?

"When you wake in the morning," Kouassi cautioned, "don't be disappointed if the food is still there. Remember, your father is an ancestor now. He can't really eat. But he can take in the food's essence. That will be enough."

I thanked Kouassi with a rush of affection for his message. I'd known this gentle man for nearly fifteen years and only now realized the depth of his friendship. Kouassi wanted to bring my father to me, a mourning son far from home and family, and this desire had given him his dream. What I didn't say was that Kouassi's words didn't ring true. My father had barely noticed my son, hadn't even called for days after the birth of his first grandchild.

I listened to Nathaniel's whistle on the other side of Amenan's compound—he and his friends were back to building a little house made from discarded mud bricks. How quickly he'd entered into the life of the village. Knowing that the Beng believe the dead exist invisibly among the living, I found it comforting to think of my father's spirit hovering in our compound, finally able to appreciate Nathaniel. Leaning into the fiction of it all, I could believe my father was finally able to openly express affection, from the emotional safety of the afterlife.

Kouassi stood to leave, then stopped and, resting on his cane, concluded with, "*Wurugbé* is for white and black people—in *wurugbé*, people are the same. They all live together."

≋   The next morning I observed that some creature, a sheep perhaps, or the chickens in the compound, had helped my father and N'zri Denju clean those cans of palm wine and yams, and I allowed myself to imagine my dad giving Beng food a taste and offering the spirit of Denju a thumbs-up.

The current Denju stood by my side, a book in hand, hoping for an early reading of Roald Dahl's *Danny, the Champion of the World*. I didn't need much cajoling to read a book that included the sentence "My father, without the slightest doubt, was the most marvelous and exciting father any boy ever had." While I doubted I'd ever deserve a review like that, I appreciated the sentiment. Nathaniel sat beside me as I read, and, suppressing a cough, I turned the pages and hoped we would never find ourselves divided by a rift the way my father and I had been.

Our chapter done, a wheeze in my chest sent me back to bed, though I expected little relief. In the past few days I'd developed an ache of a cough, making it difficult to sleep more than a few hours at a time.

Before I could settle under the mosquito netting, Alma called me out to the courtyard. There, Amenan was already arranging a semicircle of chairs for Yacouba and a group of young men who'd accompanied him from Kosangbé.

"What's up?" I asked Alma.

She shook her head. "I'm not really sure."

The formal greetings done, Yacouba thanked us for agreeing to provide modern chairs and a water pump for Kosangbé. He paused. "If it's possible, we would like to ask for something else. The elders would like a stereo system for the young people of the village."

"A *stereo system*?" I replied. I was beginning to feel less like a grateful guest of Bengland and a bit more like Santa Claus. Yet there must be a story behind this unexpected request. I leaned forward with great interest as Alma and I waited for our friend to provide it.

"The youths don't have anything to do in the evening," Yacouba explained, "or anywhere to go to amuse themselves. Farming is so hard. Why shouldn't they move to M'Bahiakro or Bouaké?"

Alma and I had noticed during our recent visits that Kosangbé had shrunk. Yacouba said that nearly all the losses had been young men and women leaving for the larger towns and cities. "And it's not easy to convince a family from another village to offer a daughter in marriage to a Kosangbé man," he continued.

I nodded at the thought of a young Beng woman's reluctance to move to such a tiny, backward place, even if Kosangbé was the most powerful of all Beng villages, ritually speaking.

"With a new water pump, and comfortable chairs for visiting elders, the reputation of our village will rise. And a weekly dance party would help keep the young people in the village, and make marriage negotiations easier, too."

"But there's no electricity in Kosangbé," Alma said. "How could you use a stereo?"

Yacouba grinned, sensing his logic was working on us. "We already have a gas-powered generator. It can be adapted to run the tape deck of a stereo system."

Alma and I whispered together. "What do you think?" she asked.

"It does make a kind of crazy sense." I loved the idea of dance parties tempting potential brides, but I didn't have to say anything else, I could see that Alma was convinced too.

"Yes, let's do it."

We turned to Yacouba, and I said, "We think this is a good idea."

"*Ka nuwalé* Amwé, *ka nuwalé* Kouadio," Yacouba replied, followed by the young men. We all stood to shake hands in the typical Beng fashion, our bodies half bent at the waist, leaning forward, left hand crossing the chest and touching the right biceps in a show of respect. When we sat down, Yacouba produced a piece of paper and said, "*Bon*, I don't know much about this, but the youths have given me this list of what components to buy. They say the best tape deck is a Sony."

ALMA: THE FIRST TWELVE MONTHS OF LIFE

Philip awoke from a long nap in the afternoon, his hands trembling, saying he felt weak and dizzy. Instead of eating dinner, he crawled back into bed; by eight o'clock he was asleep again.

"Amwé, don't worry. I'm sure it's not serious," Amenan reassured me. But she reassured me so often I worried even more.

I knew Philip struggled with his father's death, his guilt that he hadn't attended the funeral in North Carolina. I felt guilty too—if we hadn't come to Africa, my husband could have been at his father's side. Philip must have felt haunted even through the various stages of his father's village funeral ceremonies.

"Don't think about it," Amenan insisted again. "Promise me you won't think about it."

"But why not?" I asked.

"If you keep thinking about Kouadio's sickness, you might fall sick too."

As I mulled over the intriguing possibility that thoughts were contagious, Amenan sent her younger sister Ti to fetch Ajengé, a diviner who lived in a nearby compound. Ti returned with a jaunty young man sporting a beige beret, and I found it difficult to balance his appearance with his calling until, with quiet authority, he asked Amenan and me a few questions about Philip's symptoms. Then he requested a cup of cold water, which he poured in a bucket with some herbs that he'd brought along.

"When Kouadio wakes up," he instructed me, "give him a few drops of the herbal water to drink. Then we'll see what sickness it is—it's hard to know now, since he's asleep."

I thanked the healer, and soon after he left, Augustin and Bertin dropped by, fresh from the worktable they'd set up on the outskirts of the village. They had finished up the day transcribing the tape I'd recorded of the funeral for Philips's father, and now they were ambling from compound to compound, greeting people, gathering village news. When told of Ajengé's recent visit, Bertin nodded thoughtfully and said, "He's the most powerful of all the Beng diviners. He's been divining since he was two or three years old."

"Iih?"

"Whatever's wrong with Kouadio," Augustin added, "Ajengé will find the right medicines."

Later, after checking on Nathaniel's sleeping form in the bed beside ours, I put away the day's clothes by lantern light until I heard the front door of our house creak open. Straddling the doorway between our two small rooms stood Amenan, one hand oddly glowing.

"Here's some incense, Amwé," she whispered. "It's to chase away the spirit of Kouadio's father."

"Iihhh?"

"He might be what's causing Kouadio's trembling," she confided, then tiptoed out.

≋   The next morning, Amenan greeted me with bad news: "Matatu's not better."

"Now what?" I sighed, afraid to hear details.

"Last night, Matatu came by and said, 'Big Sister, you were very bad when you didn't give me anything to eat this afternoon. I was hungry!' I'd given him a snack a little earlier, but he wanted more and I refused. So he returned to complain. I told him it's not my responsibility to feed him. I was nice enough to give him anything."

"Of course," I sympathized, silently admiring my friend for her courage in standing up to Matatu.

"The problem is," Amenan continued, "he doesn't stay at his mother's house long enough to eat. He just wanders around the village."

"You should be careful," I warned her. "He might try to hurt you if he thinks you should feed him."

"I'm not afraid of him," Amenan countered, "he can only hurt people in his family."

I nodded, relieved by Amenan's reminder that among the Beng, witchcraft worked only with relatives bound by maternal ties. Yet a nagging doubt remained. Would a madman like Matatu follow the cultural script?

"Still, he isn't improving on his own," Amenan observed. "We should fetch that Ghanaian healer, so Matatu can start treatment."

Thank goodness that Germain had convinced Matatu's family to try traditional medicine for his illness, but before I could reply, Yacouba's familiar deep voice interrupted us. "Amwé, Amenan, good morning."

We exchanged greetings, and after explaining that he'd come for Asagbé's weekly market day, Yacouba asked after Philip.

"He was sick yesterday, but I'm sure he'll be up soon," I replied, hoping that stating this wish would make it so.

"A kunlia," Yacouba commiserated, eyebrows wrinkled. Then he glanced at the worktable in front of me under our palm-leaf veranda. A paperback copy of Frank and Theresa Caplan's *First Twelve Months of Life* lay face up.

"What's that?" Yacouba asked, perhaps intrigued by the smiling white mother and baby on the cover.

"It's a book that shows what babies learn, month by month," I explained.

"Let me see," Yacouba insisted and started flipping through the pages until another photo caught his eye.

"This baby is happy—it's well fed!" He paused, then flipped to another photo. "Look at this baby nursing." His brows crinkled. "What's this one doing?"

I regarded the photo: an infant slid along the floor. "She's just creeping," I said, "she hasn't learned to walk yet. Why?"

"She's slithering like a snake, Amwé," Yacouba nearly whispered. "This is evil."

"Oh?"

"Crawling with the belly up in the air is fine. But only snakes should slither like this one, with their belly on the ground," Yacouba explained. "I'd never let my child creep like that. It's a bad omen."

Yacouba quickly turned the page and chuckled at the picture of a baby holding a spoon, her face slathered with porridge. "This one is making a mess of eating!"

"Mmm, I remember when N'zri Denju used to eat like that."

"And my children, too." Yacouba paused. "I guess babies are the same everywhere."

Yacouba flipped the page to a sitting toddler gazing in the mirror. Frowning, he said, "This child isn't old enough to walk well, but he's looking at himself. This isn't good."

"Why not?" I asked.

"If he doesn't like his face, he'll return to *wurugbé*."

"You mean the child could die from looking in a mirror?" I asked.

"Of course. Babies this young are always thinking about *wurugbé*," Yacouba stated plainly. "They miss their old life back there, and if they don't like something in this life, they decide to go back."

Then Yacouba tensed up at the photo of an open-mouthed baby laughing at the camera. I couldn't see what bothered my friend.

"Don't you see, Amwé?" Yacouba shook his head. "This child has too many teeth."

"What do you mean?"

"He's barely over a year. Maybe he isn't *even* a year. A baby that age shouldn't have so many teeth. It's another bad omen."

"What do you mean, 'bad omen'?" I asked.

"You know, *tété*," Yacouba replied under his breath. "Someone in the family must have died soon after that picture was taken. Probably one of the baby's grandparents." He shook his head again.

"But how do you know?"

"There's a time for everything, Amwé," Yacouba explained. "A baby should get at least *one* tooth before it learns to walk, otherwise it's *tété*. But it shouldn't get a *full* set of teeth before it learns to walk—that's *tété*, too. Same with talking. A baby shouldn't say its first word before it gets its first teeth, otherwise it's *tété*."

I started scribbling like mad while Yacouba continued, "Plus, all babies should be born *trobi trobi*—you know, toothless. If a baby's born with teeth, that's *tété*. In the old days, we would have killed a baby like that—otherwise, one of the grandparents would die. You know the mats we put our babies on, when they lie down outside?"

I nodded.

"Have you ever noticed where women put the mats to dry after washing them?"

I admitted I'd never paid much attention.

"Well, women usually dry the mats anywhere," Yacouba explained. "But if a woman has a baby who hasn't cut his first tooth yet, she always takes care to dry the baby's mats by spreading them on the ground—she never dries them up on a rooftop or a clothesline. If she did, the baby would cut his first tooth on top."

"*Ah-heh*," I said, and nodded at the book, inviting him to turn the next page, all the while chiding myself not only for assuming that women alone would find this book interesting, but for forgetting that the most ordinary-seeming of baby habits were extraordinary indeed, depending on your perspective. How hard it was at times to keep the anthropological gaze focused.

≋ I sat on a stool in a small room of Ajengé's mud-brick house as a husband and wife explained to him that their three-month-old had been crying day and night, though he didn't appear sick. They hoped the diviner could diagnose the problem and suggest a cure. Philip, always interested in the doings of the spirit world, sat beside me, suppressed a cough, and leaned in as Amenan translated.

After staring intently at a silver coin in the palm of the father's hand, Ajengé announced that the baby himself wanted two items: a white piece of cloth and a dark bracelet. In addition, the mother must stop being angry about something causing her unhappiness. Amenan—ever the village gossip—whispered that Ajengé's analysis was spot on. The baby's mother was indeed upset: newly married, she had to endure a hostile older co-wife. Plenty of fights had erupted in this household, and Amenan thought that the baby's crying was a response to all the raised tempers.

When Ajengé instructed the parents that they must together buy a white cloth and a dark bracelet for the baby, I wondered if this advice was a clever means to encourage the couple to cooperate, and allow the husband to show his commitment to his new wife. Such an act could calm her down, and her calmness might spread to the baby. Ajengé must be as good a village gossip as Amenan. Indeed, he seemed to be playing the role of family therapist.

But after the couple left and I asked Ajengé what he had known about the family's marital troubles, he protested, "I didn't know anything about the family. I don't have time to walk around the village and greet people, the way others do. I'm too busy. All I knew about the baby's family was what I saw. Do you remember the coin the father held in the palm of his hand? It worked like a mirror. It showed me the truth of what was inside the baby."

I wasn't sure if there were any secrets in a Beng village but kept this thought to myself.

In the silence, Ajengé asked how the funeral for Philip's father was proceeding, and we told him that we'd finally found a nice-sized sheep for the sacrifice that Kokora Kouassi wanted to conduct.

Ajengé nodded and then began to speak, enigmatically, about *wurugbé*—the Beng afterlife. "Every day, there are deaths and births," he said. "The number of people living here and in *wurugbé* keeps going up and down. You know who you're replacing from *wurugbé* if someone dies on the same day that you're born. Otherwise, you don't know who you're replacing."

I wasn't sure why Ajengé had brought this up, but Philip listened intently to Amenan's translation, as if it spoke to him in a way he couldn't explain.

PHILIP: WELCOMING GHOSTS

Some of the kids playing with Nathaniel had asked to hear my tape of Zagazougou, so I grabbed it off the shelf in our house, but only a few steps into the courtyard my legs gave way beneath me, as if invisible strings had been cut. Alma and Amenan rushed over as I lay there, marveling at the sudden fall: one moment walking, the next on the ground. Kofi worked his way through the circle of children and lifted me by my shoulders until I was finally able to stand. I felt so shaken I tried to joke the moment away, smiling at Nathaniel to reassure his worried face, Alma's too, and then said as I held out the tape, "*Bon*, who wants to dance to some music?"

That evening, Amenan brought Ajengé to the compound. I lay in bed, tired as usual, but I could hear their voices through the mud walls of our small house, the sound of Alma's voice replying to them. Then she came into the room, sat by the side of our bed, and said, "Ajengé brought more medicinal leaves from the forest for you. I'm supposed to simmer them in water and then wash you with the broth."

"Sure, I feel so lousy you can wash me with anything, if that's going to help this awful cough."

Alma was silent, and I could see her calculating a response. "It's not for your cough."

"Oh? Then what's it for?"

"Well, I didn't want to mention this, but Amenan thinks you're sick because your father's spirit is calling you. That's why she asked Ajengé for help. The leaves are supposed to protect you, hold you to the earth."

"You mean, they think my dad is trying to kill me?"

"No, they're worried that you're so sad, you might try to join him."

"Well, I'm sad, that's for sure, but I ain't going nowhere, don't worry about that."

"So, you don't think you need to—"

"No, let's do the treatment, it's so sweet of everyone to worry about me," I said. Alma kissed me on the forehead, then puttered around in the other room, boiling the leaves in a pot of water. As a thick vegetable smell filled the air, I returned to reading *Bones*, a novel by Chenjerai Hove about Zimbabwe's war of independence. I loved the style, a poetic combination of English and the rhythms of the Shona language. In some chapters, the ancestors spoke from the spirit world, and I certainly knew something about that.

Soon the water would cool enough so Alma could rub me down with a washcloth. I'd agreed to go through the ritual, yet if the real cause of my illness was regret, where was the cure for that?

≋ Alma, Nathaniel, and I sat at the table in the compound, sipping happily from bowls of sweet corn porridge that even I enjoyed, though my chest ached. I wiggled my toes against my sandals, against the packed dirt of the ground, but didn't necessarily feel held fast to the earth. Already I could imagine going back inside and taking a nap. Then Kokora Kouassi approached, his blind eyes facing our voices, and something about his slow, serious gait made me think that another dream might be coming.

I'd guessed right, because when he sat down on the chair Amenan had hurried over for him, he announced a dream that concerned me.

"I dreamt of Kouadio's father again, and Gbongbo Ndri."

Alma and I glanced at each other. Who was this other guy, and why was he important to Kouassi's dream?

Alma turned to Amenan, who said, "Gbongbo Ndri was the chief of Asagbé . . . four chiefs ago, when I was a child."

When Kouassi felt Amenan had explained Gbongbo Ndri's identity, he went on to say that the chief had met with my father in *wurugbé*. "Kouadio, your father says he's content in *wurugbé*, but you should stay here, among the living. Don't follow him."

I nodded my head at such a welcome dream. Wanting to believe in my father's otherworldly concern, how willing I was to hear his voice in Kouassi's words, how willing to try any method to ease my unhappiness, and I thought of a quote I'd recently copied in my notebook from Chenjerai Hove's novel: "The things of the heart cannot be read by too many people. They burn inside like a big fire which people cannot know how to put out."

"Thank you, Aba," I replied, suppressing a cough, "I will listen."

≋ I leaned back in my chair, hands off the keyboard, and paused. Through the screen door I could see Nathaniel and Bapu in the courtyard, attaching a motley collection of dead branches together with strips of vine. I couldn't yet make out what they were building and decided to wait until they were farther along before going outside to admire their handiwork. Amenan's feisty daughter Esi walked past them, hauling a pail of water, pausing to declare, "Ehhh, N'zri Denju *dangana!*" This was a new variation on Nathaniel's African name, which had immediately become popular in the compound. *Dangana* meant something like a silly or kooky fellow, and this was certainly an apt comment on Nathaniel's unconventional behavior: his American child's sense of freedom sometimes rubbed up against the Beng belief in a child's necessary deference to adults. So now our son was known as Wacky Grandfather Denju, which indeed seemed to better describe this particular six-year-old revered ancestor.

I returned to my keyboard stare, trying to resolve a difficult scene in my novel, but soon reached for my notebook instead. Another character had just come to me as if from the air, joining a list I'd been collecting in my notebook for the past month. This one was an entomologist who, after her death, decides to spend her afterlife among the ants. I scribbled down a line or two, all that I knew of her so far. With luck this mere sentence would grow, in time. What I did understand was that she didn't belong in the novel I was trying to finish. This was the start of something else, something new.

Another ghost. All these characters who'd been popping up inside me lately were ghosts: a computer hacker who plays the afterlife as a freeing virtual reality; the ghost of a car mechanic who discovers a love for audiobooks; a Mexican-American ghost obsessed with the notion of borders; and a Protestant from the nineteenth century who is shocked to find himself in an afterlife he wasn't expecting. Already I knew that these American ghosts were wandering about a Midwestern town in an afterlife that resembled the *wurugbé* of the Beng.

I'd been jotting down these budding characters even before my father died, but since his funeral ceremonies in the village, more and more arrived. With my American father in an African afterlife, now I was transposing that afterlife to an American setting. Every book I read seemed to be pointing me in this direction: in a collection of African short fiction, a line from a story by Kojo Laing seemed to shout out: "Spirit is the indivisible atom, the atom's atom's atom!"

Now I wondered if maybe I should put aside, just for a few days, the novel I'd been working on for so long, and offer a stretch of emotional space to welcome these new characters. I sat with my notebook on my lap, waiting to see which book would win the claim on my time. Outside the screen door, a line of goats walked past in a steady swaying gait, nosing about for any edible discarded thing.

≋ Scrunched in the back seat of the car beside Alma and Nathaniel sat Ajei, the Ghanaian healer who'd agreed to take on the case of Matatu's illness, and beside me Kofi warned of especially impressive upcoming potholes, though I could easily see them myself. The French word for a narrow little trail like this is *piste*, but a true *piste* boasted superhighway status compared to this horror of crevices and fault lines that constantly required maneuvering, and the dirt banks on either side of this *piste* stood close enough to scrape the car. Whenever patches of sandy soil sucked the wheels to a stop, Kofi and I pushed the car from behind, while Alma gunned the engine and the healer and Nathaniel stood safely off to the side.

Too often we came upon a four- or five-foot-high termite mound in the middle of the trail that I had to squeeze around—sometimes with two wheels high on the edge of one of the raised banks. I had to apply constant attention to the slightest trick and trap, and the trail stretched on and on as if it would never end. I'd already driven back and forth to the healer's village days earlier, to ask for his help and offer him a chicken as a sign of respect. Now here I was again on this nasty seven-kilometer stretch. Perhaps this was a minor hell assigned to me for all my sins when I drove a cab one long-ago summer in New York City.

Finally, after emptying everyone out once again for another termite mound so the car wouldn't tip over when it angled against the trail's raised bank, some tenuous constraint snapped inside me. With the latest obstruction safely behind us, and the car full once more, off we drove. But now added to the dutiful *rrrrrr* of the engine rose from me first a murmur, then a full-throated string of the worst insults in any language that I could summon, a rising and falling, a rolling along of a Frenbenglish twisted eloquence that surprised even me. Once started, with no internal ignition key to switch off my running road-trip commentary, I couldn't stop.

Alma normally would have bored a hole in the back of my head for this string of curses I let loose within hearing range of Nathaniel, but this was one of those moments that *demanded* cursing, a protest against this reprehensible road. In the rearview mirror I saw Nathaniel hunched over his drawing pad, pen carefully applied to the page, deep in his own world of art. Even if he listened, he'd have to learn these words some time in his life, and what better pedagogical moment could there be than the provocation of this road? On and on it perversely re-revealed its unique features, as if egging me on.

I would have protested Philip's string of curses let loose within hearing range of Nathaniel, but I suspected that my husband's foul mouth was less a complaint against this path-in-the-guise-of-a-road and more an outpouring of pent-up sadness at his father's death back home. So I took the diversionary tactic of talking to the healer about his life. I posed questions in English to Kofi, who graciously translated to the healer in Fante, then back in English—and Nathaniel had the rare experience of actually understanding what was said around him.

The topic piqued his interest, and at times he suggested new questions. At first, since the subject of the interview was so—well, adult—the mother in me didn't want to upset Nathaniel. But my young son seemed to have developed his own anthropological curiosity. After all, he'd already accepted his new village name of Denju and being hailed as a reincarnation of an important clan ancestor.

"Do you know why Matatu went mad?" I asked the healer.

"I do know," the healer said quietly, after Kofi translated, "otherwise I couldn't cure him. I can't discuss it now. But I've spoken with Matatu . . ."

"Ah, *bon?*" I commented, surprised. I hadn't heard about any recent visits the healer had paid to our village.

"I heard Matatu speaking to me in my mind, just as a diviner would do. I could hear that Matatu speaks nonsense . . ."

Nathaniel looked up from his drawing pad. "What medicine will the healer use?"

I repeated the question to Kofi, who translated without having to raise his voice. By now, Philip had reverted to muttering.

"The same I use for any patient, though I have a very strong blend of herbs and plants for people who are very mad."

"*Ah-heh,*" I said noncommittally. I'd expected some ritual approach to reposition Matatu in his social universe—not an herbal cure. Maybe the healer sensed my skepticism, for he added, "I can cure a lot of other diseases, not just madness. But I also tell a patient if I don't know the cure for whatever disease they may have."

Nathaniel joined in, and Kofi translated, "How come Matatu is crazy?"

"I might find that a disease is caused by witchcraft," Ajei hinted ominously. "Then, one night while I'm alone in my house, I beg the witches to reverse the spell. I ask what they need, and I buy back the spell from them with whatever they ask for as payment. It might be a sheep, some money, or alcohol—or just a chicken or some eggs. Last night, I talked with the witches who bewitched Matatu."

Ajei paused while this statement sank in. "I met the witches," the healer continued, "and they said they wanted money, nothing else."

"How come they didn't get arrested?" Nathaniel asked me quietly.

"I think the healer meant they met invisibly. Like in dreams." Accustomed to hearing of his grandfather appearing in Kokora Kouassi's dreams, Nathaniel nodded and once again bent over his drawing pad.

"The witches said they'd need 200 CFAs—all in small change," the healer concluded. "To pay them, I'll give the money to the children in the village—one small coin to each child—and the witches will undo the spell on Matatu. Then, when I give Matatu my herbal medicine, the witches will allow the medicine to work."

"But who *are* the witches?" Nathaniel asked.

The healer remained silent for a few seconds after Kofi translated, then said quietly, "Actually, the witch responsible for Matatu's madness is his own mother."

I should have been able to predict this accusation, since Beng witchcraft always operates within the maternal line. Still, I was impressed. Ajei must have lived long enough in the Beng region to be able to chart their paths of sorcery. I glanced at my son. What might Nathaniel make of this unexpected, perhaps unthinkable answer? A new set of especially bumpy bumps claimed our attention, and we were left to ponder the upsetting news in our solitude.

≋ When we finally returned to Asagbé, Nathaniel tugged at Philip's shirt and said, "Dad, look at what I did," with an open-faced enthusiasm. We both looked down at his sketchpad.

The page bristled with nervous, jagged lines, each one running from left to right, line after line, repeating down to the bottom edge. Philip stared, clearly trying to figure out what it was so he could praise it.

"It's . . ." he hesitated.

"It's a seismograph," Nathaniel said.

"A . . . what?"

"A seismograph. It's a souvenir of the road, the bad road."

We looked again at the drawing. I'd been so intent on my interview with the healer that I'd barely noticed Nathaniel's determined concentration. With the drawing pad on his lap, he'd applied the pen lightly to the page and let the road do his work for him . . . and charted very twist, turn, rattle, and shake we'd all suffered through. Seismograph! Where did he get that word? It certainly hadn't been in any of the phrases Philip had employed while driving. Yet maybe my husband's extended stretch of curses were recorded too on this drawing pad, in some pre-alphabetic stenography.

"Amazing. Thank you, Grandfather Denju," Philip replied as he held the pad and examined that skittish map as if it were a record of all this summer's surprises.

≋   "*Aba*, don't go, no no no no no!" the tiny girl shouted to her father as he rose to leave our compound. I'd just given some medicine to her baby brother.

The girl turned to me. "I want to go to the fields with Papa. Maybe your son can go with me. Can N'zri Denju come too? We can both go together. Won't that be nice? I really want to go with Papa!" Her father tied to reassure her that he'd return soon from the fields, but his daughter kept crying.

"She sure can speak well, can't she?" Amenan commented beside me. "She's barely three, and listen to her. Her name is Amani."

I nodded. Any Amani—a child born after twins—was considered more than a handful, but Amenan felt compelled to point out the obvious. "So she must be a witch."

Amenan turned to the girl to reassure her. "He'll be back soon," she said. "He's just going to harvest some new corn, and when he returns, he'll give you some."

"No, he's gone to get new *rice*," Amani corrected Amenan, "not new *corn*. He'll come back with *rice* and give me some!"

Amenan and I both chuckled. Amani was certainly an impressive little talker . . . as well as quite moody. After she sat down to pout, her glum mood seemed infectious as Amenan's grown daughter, pregnant Evelyne, walked across the compound, head downcast.

"She looks depressed," I said quietly to Amenan.

"Her big sister's done a terrible thing," Amenan confided.

"Akissi?" I asked, then corrected myself—after marrying a Muslim, she'd changed her name. "I mean, Tahan?"

"*Ah-heh*. You know what a temper Tahan has," Amenan said. That was certainly no secret. Though Tahan was a caring attentive mother to her infant son, Sassandra, she was always slapping her undersized eight-year-old son, Meda. One day, when she'd beaten him longer than usual, Nathaniel was so outraged at this mistreatment of one of his buddies that he went up to Tahan, tapped her on the shoulder, and delivered a shaming lecture that, although she didn't know a word of English, she certainly understood. Tahan had laughed off Nathaniel's critique, but I was proud of my son's bravery—and in the face of my own cowardly silence, no less.

"This time, Tahan really went too far," Amenan said. "When you were in Abidjan, she and Evelyne had a huge fight. Evelyne's been cooking for the family every day, but one night she was too tired to make dinner. I asked Tahan to cook but she refused. Evelyne got mad at her, then Tahan became furious and swore on the Earth."

Amenan paused so I could take in the gravity of this sin. If the Earth spirits carried out the curse during Evelyne's labor, it could kill her.

"We'll have to hold a trial for Tahan's having cursed Evelyne in the name of the Earth. I'm sure she'll have to sacrifice at least a chicken to undo the curse. Maybe even a goat. Without that, Evelyne's delivery could be trouble. And Tahan will be blamed, *vraiment*."

The story confirmed my worst feelings about Tahan. Refusing to relieve her tired, pregnant sister was bad enough; cursing her was really over the top. Perhaps she was jealous. Evelyne's husband Kwamela was a tailor in M'Bahiakro, a likely path toward a more prosperous life that was now closed to Tahan. Even so, her behavior couldn't restrain me from judging harshly. While I clucked in disapproval, Amenan resumed her lament. "I'm going to ask an elder in the village to judge the case right away. We can't wait—we have to do everything we can to make sure Evelyne's delivery goes well."

Amenan stood silently, and I felt a pang of sympathy at how my friend had aged, in the worried lines of her face. With Kofi gone the past few years, and with her mother lost in a quiet depression that kept her sitting most days in the doorway to her mud-brick house, gazing at the doings of the compound without comment, Amenan had become the head of the household, responsible for the negotiation of any family trouble.

≋ "You two are really working hard," I commented as Dieudonné used a triangle of cardboard to pour shelled peanuts into a large burlap bag that his wife Adèle shook up and down.

I had been recording so many interviews that Bertin and Augustin were nearly overwhelmed with their transcription work, so I'd recently added Dieudonné as my third assistant. Though he had a junior high school education, he'd returned to the village to become a farmer, and he was enthusiastic about helping me observe babies more systematically. Infants, whether awake or asleep, were carried by so many people, and so often, that they must lead very active social lives. Could I add some numbers to that hunch? I trained Dieudonné to spend hours watching select babies and recording their minute-to-minute interactions on time sheets I created. Soon we'd tally up the count of his initial observations to see if they supported my impressions.

"The machine has already shelled the peanuts," Adèle explained, pointing to a large machine across the courtyard. "But after it separates the nuts from the shells, it drops them on the ground and they all get mixed together. So we have to separate them. After we shake them in the bag, the shells float up to the top and the nuts stay on the bottom."

"Where'd you get the machine?" I asked.

Dieudonné said, "I rented it from a guy in Bongalo. He charges us 150 CFAs a bag to shell our peanuts. I can make a lot more money selling the peanuts if they're shelled."

"But it's worth it," Adèle added. "From all the work we're doing now, we'll have seven bags of peanuts and we'll sell them in Bouaké."

"Will you make a good profit?"

Dieudonné replied, "Decent enough. I'll save more money by bringing the bags myself. It would cost us 1,000 CFAs a bag to ship them."

"Yih, that's a lot," I commented.

"The selling price changes a lot," Dieudonné continued. "Right now peanuts are selling for 165 CFAs a kilo in Bouaké. In a few months, it'll be the height of the harvest, and the price can go as low as 100 a kilo. But in March and April, peanuts are rare, and the price can go as high as 250. So you see, there's some money to be made . . ."

Unlike coffee, I thought bitterly. André had recently told me that, like so many others in the village, he had abandoned harvesting his coffee trees because the price had fallen so low, and he'd switched to growing rice. Nodding, I thought that in the future, Dieudonné and Adèle would never again have to rent that shelling machine, since the Asagbé elders had finally agreed upon a project for our book royalties: a large mill versatile enough not only to shell peanuts but also to hull rice and process coffee beans and cacao, for the benefit of all the villagers. Soon we would travel to Abidjan to begin the process of purchasing the mill, with the help of the American embassy funds. I didn't look forward to the inevitable paperwork.

≋ "I don't know paper," the elder conceded, sitting with a group of old men beneath the sprawling roots of the kapok tree that sheltered all village meetings. "Here, Little Brother, you read this."

He handed the sheet of paper to the high school student standing in the shadow of the tree. Sporting khaki trousers and a pressed navy polo, this teen-ager served as the formal speaker for his fellow students. He read the agenda aloud, and the elder then addressed the group of old men with the important news that five Beng high school seniors from around the country had just passed the French-style *Bac* exam; in the fall, they would enter the national uni-versity in Abidjan. This year's crop of incoming college students was a huge in-crease from our first time in the country, when only one Beng student, Kouadio Pascal, attended the university.

Another elder turned to Germain, standing next to the seated group: "May god bless the students who passed the test!"

Germain then repeated the blessing to the students' speaker, who in turn re-peated it to the two dozen Beng junior and senior high school students behind him who'd converged on Asagbé for today's meeting.

"Thank you," said the students' speaker, and the other students repeated their gratitude.

Just recently, I'd observed a graduation ceremony at the small elementary school in Asagbé. All the students in sixth grade had taken a national test that would announce whether they passed sixth grade. Only thirteen out of thirty-six students who had passed the test had done so at a high enough level to proceed to junior high school.

This honor would come at a steep cost. Those students would leave Beng-land to attend school in another town, where they'd board with a relative all week; if they were lucky, their families could scrape together the bus fare so they could return to the village one weekend a month. In the face of these sta-tistics, my assistant Dieudonné's junior high school diploma was impressive; the fact that the five students would continue at the university level seemed a miracle.

"Now, Elder Brother, I have something else to say," the students' speaker said.

"Yes?" Germain asked.

"We'd like the elders to allow more children from the villages to attend school," the young man said. "Right now, not many do. If more Beng children go to school, the region can develop."

The elders nodded, some of them the same Beng elders who had adamantly opposed Western education in any guise; back in 1979, we'd heard, they had even conducted a sacrifice requesting the ancestors to prevent any student from passing to the next grade level. Now their reversal was terribly timed: while the Beng finally embraced the promise of schooling, the country's economy con-tinued its downward course.

My last patient walked away gingerly, the bandage on her foot covering a nasty sore I'd doused with antibiotic cream—a round sore surrounding a pus-filled wound, like so many inflected cuts I'd been treating these days. Though I'd been at it for hours, I stood beside the table, unwilling to pack away the various medicines I'd been dispensing, and waited to see if anyone else might drop by.

I preferred the work's distraction. The rituals of my father's Beng funeral had ended, including the sacrifice of a sheep whose various parts we'd contributed to Amenan's and the neighboring compounds. But the loss of my father lingered, as well as my shame that I hadn't been with him when he'd died. I'd even lashed out at Alma, blaming her for bringing me back to Africa at the worst possible time, but of course the decision had been mine. And then I felt guilty for my continuing sadness, since there was far greater misery in the village. A few children had died of malnutrition this summer, and some young mothers had confided to Alma that they worried their children might never leave the village for a better life. The old chief of the village had recently passed away, and everyone was hunkered down for an increased bout of witchcraft—the Beng people's anxieties always increased whenever someone powerful died. Even worse was the prospect that the country's ailing president, Houphouët-Boigny, who was hospitalized in France, might soon die. With no clear line of succession, who knew what troubles might follow his passing? At times, Asagbé seemed to be suffering from a communal bout of depression.

At least I'd recovered sufficiently from my off-and-on bed-ridden exhaustion of recent weeks, which Alma felt convinced was pneumonia. She'd even traveled to M'Bahiakro to describe my symptoms to a doctor, and brought back medicine for me. At times, all I could do was cough while flattened against the foam mattress, barely able to move while paging through the last of the books I had brought to read this summer: *The Magic Mountain*. Earlier in our stay I'd held off because I wasn't in the mood for a hefty bear of a book, but confined to bed I soon regretted the decision to wait, since a remote tuberculosis sanatorium in the Swiss Alps wasn't an ideal fictional locale, considering the state of my own lungs. Every hack and chuff of mine boded further ill, and I'd found less and less sympathy for Hans Castorp, whose mere low-grade fever enabled him to stick around and indulge in a seemingly endless mope over his fellow patient, Madame Chauchat. You're not even *sick*, I had muttered at him, as if his finally leaving that sanatorium would improve my own health.

No one else showed for my mini-doctoring, so I began hauling the various ointments, anti-malaria pills, aspirin, and bandages back into our house. On one return to the table, I noticed Nathaniel at the edge of our compound, clearing away the brush with a machete. As far as I knew, he hadn't asked to attempt this job; he simply picked up a machete from somewhere and, leaning over, swung the blade before him in a spot-on imitation of the loping style of the adults who usually performed this task. We'd been living in the village for only a few months, yet I could imagine the path into Beng culture that Nathaniel might follow if we were to stay longer.

Still, a machete was a machete, and he was just a little kid, so I walked beside my son, admiring his work aloud, resisting the impulse to take the sharp blade from him, limiting myself to a "Be careful" now and then. Weren't we all taking in more of Beng culture than we'd perhaps ever imagined? Our son seen as a reincarnated ancestor, my father in residence in *wurugbé*, and Alma and I had certainly internalized Beng notions of obligation—though with so much need, how much of a difference would our efforts finally make?

We'd just returned from another trek to Abidjan, where we'd wandered, lost at first, through a busy industrial landscape near the city in search of the factory that produced those plastic chairs the Kosangbé elders coveted. We ordered fifty in a deep blue color from a bemused manager, arranged for the delivery, and paid for everything in advance. We'd also managed to make a side trip to the supplier of the mill that the Asagbé elders had decided upon, and gathered forms from the American embassy so we could receive matching funds for the project. Finally, with Bertin's help, we found just the right components for the stereo system his childhood village had requested in the hopes that weekly dance parties at Kosangbé would make it a more attractive home for young brides from other villages. As Nathaniel continued clearing the brush beside me, nearly done with his circling of the compound, I couldn't help smiling at the thought that part of our book royalties would pay for advanced Japanese electronics in the service of shoring up the demographics of a small African village.

I smiled, too, at the memory of our return to Bengland from that jaunt, when we'd stopped first at the village of Bongalo, to stock up at their market on fresh vegetables, rice, and dried fish that we'd share with Amenan's family. Since Bongalo was Jean's village, once finished with shopping we ambled over to his compound, and saw him sitting outside on the low stoop of the front door to his small mud-brick home. A semicircle of children sat before him, and on his lap rested one of the two volumes of the encyclopedia we'd given him as a gift. Jean rose at the sight of us, and we exchanged greetings and village news. Then he pointed to his young visitors and explained, "These children like to come to my compound and have me read to them from the encyclopedias. It helps them in their studies." He'd been in the middle of an entry on the solar system, a picture of Saturn taking up one half of a page, so we said our farewells and left him to the satisfactions of his tutoring, but not before he eyed the children, raised one arm high, a finger pointing to the sky as if invoking the assent of a higher power, and said, "Remember, pay attention. These two books contain all the knowledge of the world—it's all here for you!"

Beside me, Nathaniel paused, wiped sweat from his forehead. Clearing brush was hard work.

≋ Alma was off somewhere interviewing a young mother, and who knew where Nathaniel might be, scrambling around the village with his friends. Sitting at my desk, puzzling over Gladys, the mother in my novel who kept trying on different identities, I heard Matatu stroll into the compound and greet a circle of Amenan's extended family lazing about, chatting and enjoying the rest day. Unfortunately, Ajei's efforts had failed with Matatu, who'd refused to cooperate with the healer. Matatu was, after all, the *premier ministre*, much too important for "African medicine." Only Western medicine would do.

I listened to his voice mingling with the others and anticipated his eventual appearance at the screen door, where he'd peer at me and take another photo with his cigarette-box contraption. If I were lucky, that would be enough. Otherwise, I'd have to endure another session of his ministerial adventures and proclamations, or another accounting of the contents of his magic bag, until he spent himself and wandered off to find another of his constituents.

On the other hand, I thought, maybe a visit from Matatu would give my writing the spark I needed. I was having trouble with this mad mother of a character, not sure what she'd do next in the kitchen while her children sat frightened at the table. I paused, amazed at how similar Gladys and Matatu were. How could I have not noticed this before?

Outside, there was the murmur of Matatu's voice, the bursts of laughter at what must have been his wild assertions of power and dominion, and, increasingly, his rising tone of anger. Then, stone silence. Not a good silence. I pushed back my chair, walked to the screen door.

Matatu held the sharp edge of his broken scissors against Ti's neck. No one moved, all eyes on that blade. "I am the prime minister! I am the prime minister!" Matatu shouted. "*C'est vrai?*" Her neck arched back, her eyes on him, Ti managed to say through pressed lips, "*Oui*, you are the prime minister."

With a satisfied grunt he stepped away from her, bent down, and rummaged through that bag of his. And everyone else went back to chatting, as if nothing had happened. I couldn't believe it, still feeling the adrenaline rush inside me. Was it a stunned, nervous reaction, or did they feel a madman's actions had no consequence?

Moments later Matatu crouched a few feet away from the screen door. He leaned over a small wooden box—what he must have been searching for in his bag—and with his scissors he began dismantling it, piece by piece. While he chopped he sang a little improvised song in an eerie, childlike voice, and I realized the lyric had only one word: "Denju, Denju, Denju, Denju."

He hacked away at what was by then a former box, hacked it down to chips, still singing my son's name while I watched in hypnotized horror, watched Matatu as if he were slicing my child with every arc and sweep of his arm. Where was Nathaniel, anyway?

Off somewhere on his usual adventures in the village, and safely far from this compound. But what if he came back, this minute or the next? I shook off my shock, stood up, and reached for a length of wood, the table leg that never was, which Nathaniel had collected from the carpenter. No way would Matatu get near my real, flesh-and-blood son. By now, Matatu had swept the tiny wooden pieces into a cupped hand and returned them to his bag. Who knew what other transformations they might go through in his mind before he was done with them?

Matatu stood, slung the bag over his shoulder, and left the compound, and suddenly my absent son was not so safe. Where was he? I rushed out of the house and saw Ti and Kouadio and the rest staring, stunned, at Matatu's departure. They had seen what I had seen.

"Where is Denju, we have to find Denju," I said. They all hurried away in different directions while I locked the door to our house, and then I realized that Alma was off at an interview, with no idea what Matatu might be capable of. I could imagine him catching a glimpse of her, sitting on a bark-cloth mat, probably with a young mother and child, maybe chatting about Beng babies and reincarnation, and then he approached her, that odd smile on his lips . . .

Who should I search for, who protect first?

ALMA: MYSTICAL MUSICAL CHAIRS

Dieudonné showed Amenan and me the charts where he'd meticulously recorded every activity that he could observe in babies he'd sat with for two-and-a-quarter hours at a stretch.

"It looks like over half the babies nursed anywhere from two to . . . five times each during those short periods," I noted.

Dieudonné adjusted his chubby fourteen-month-old daughter Hallelujah on his lap. "Is that surprising?"

"*C'est normal*," Amenan chimed in.

"Well, it's a lot more than what most American mothers do," I replied. Pediatric nurses and doctors often cautioned nursing mothers to set a rigid schedule and breastfeed no more than once every three or four hours, to avoid spoiling babies. But Beng mothers don't follow a schedule because, since babies are ancestors come back to life they often miss their previous existence and are tempted to return. Keeping them attached to this world meant luring them with every source of satisfaction one could offer a baby, and of course the first pleasure lay in the breast. Now Dieudonné's observations were putting numbers on this worldview.

I thanked him and gathered his latest data sheets, and Amenan and I started to return to her compound.

"Dieudonné's such an attentive father," I observed.

"More than you know," Amenan said.

"Oh?"

"Hallelujah's not his oldest child." Amenan paused. "His first wife died."

"My god!" I blurted out.

"When she died, she had a toddler and a nursing baby, only three months old. Dieudonné carried that baby on his back a lot."

"But what about—"

"Breastfeeding? The very night his wife died, Tahan nursed the baby. She and Dieudonné's wife had given birth the same week, and Tahan had plenty of milk."

I grimaced inside with shame at my initial secret hesitancy about hiring Dieudonné because he was an evangelical Christian. He belonged to a recently established Protestant congregation in Asagbé that had become increasingly divisive toward the animists, Catholics, and Muslims who lived in the village, threatening the ecumenical religious attitude I'd long admired about the Beng. Yet Dieudonné's easygoing nature had allayed my fears; now I saw another side to his nurturing soul.

As we neared Amenan's compound, she continued, "It's hard to raise very young children whose mother died. If you don't have a good heart, the children will die. If you insult them, they'll get a fever—"

Just then, as we entered Amenan's compound I saw an agitated Philip atypically locking the wooden door to our mud-brick house.

"What's up?" I asked.

I listened, nearly numb, as Philip quickly recounted two frightening scissors incidents. "Who knows what Matatu's planning?" he blurted out. "We've got to find Nathaniel!"

I could barely speak. Of all the dangers I had anticipated and planned for before leaving for Africa, nothing approached the possibility that a madman might attack my son.

Taking me by the hand, Philip explained that Amenan's family had already fanned out through the village in opposite directions, searching the sandal tracks that Nathaniel and his pals made on the dusty paths. But before Philip and I were able to join them, our son, Bapu, Meda, and the rest returned safe to the compound, accompanied by Amenan's husband Kofi and her brother Kofi Ba.

"Shhhh," Philip said to me, and I understood that we should say nothing to Nathaniel for the moment—no need to frighten him. Oblivious to the danger he might have been in, Nathaniel started playing a game that looked something like tag with his friends. My eyes swerved in every direction as casually as possible while Philip asked Kofi to send word to Germain about what had just happened.

Soon a gathering of village elders convened in Amenan's compound. When Germain repeated to them what Matatu had done to Ti, and the ominous way he threatened our son, a consensus was quickly reached. Matatu's erratic and violent behavior had spread beyond the confines of his own family. Breaking the Beng rules of madness meant no one in the village could feel safe. He would have to be sent back to the psychiatric hospital in Bouaké.

We kept Nathaniel beside us for the rest of the day. Later that evening, Amenan told us that when Matatu got word of the plan, he protested so loudly that he had to be restrained and tied up again. I thanked her for the news, but still knew that none of us would feel calm until he was finally taken from the village.

≋ Soon enough we'd leave the village ourselves. Paging through my spiral-bound notebooks filled with jottings, I worried that I hadn't collected enough material. True, I'd produced thousands of pages filled with observations of babies' waking and sleeping hours, women's comments on why they put this or that necklace on their child, and diviners' mystical explanations for the seemingly strange behavior of infants and the cycle of reincarnations. I understood that women bathed, decorated, and bejeweled their babies not only to attract babysitting girls, freeing the mothers to do the fourteen hours of work that claimed their days, but also to keep their infants held to this world. I smiled at the thought of the Beng phrase for baby babble, *wurugbé jowolé*—the language of the afterlife.

But was there enough humanity, enough of individuals' lives, to give a rich texture to the book I wanted to write? As I leafed through the two oversized notebooks filled with Bertin's and Augustin's translations of the hundreds of interviews I'd conducted in Beng and French, I glanced up and said to Amenan, "I'd like to collect more life histories, to get a longer sense of women's experiences as mothers. Who else do you think I should talk to?"

"If you talk to Grandmother Sopi, you'll know more about women's suffering," she said.

I remembered Sopi from our second stay in Bengland, and the persistent cut on her leg that Philip had treated. He'd tried every curative cream the pharmacist in M'Bahiakro had recommended, but the cut stubbornly refused to heal—though it never worsened, either. Sopi had possessed an almost uncanny ability to endure without complaint the hardship of her wound, which had lasted for years. Now Amenan's comment made me wonder what further sufferings the old woman had withstood.

"You know, Big Sister," I said, "I asked my doctor back in America about that cut of Sopi's. He said it sounded like the wound was ulcerated, and that's why it never healed, even after all the different creams we tried."

"*Ihhh?*" Amenan responded skeptically. "That may be, but most people here say it was witchcraft. When you ask about her children, you'll see what I mean."

Two days later, Sopi sat beside us in Amenan's compound, clutching a small square of softened brown bark cloth, and listening attentively as Amenan explained that I'd like to know the story of her children.

"Yes, Amwé, I'll tell you everything," the old woman agreed quietly.

"I've heard that your son has died recently," I began. "I'm very sorry, I offer my condolences. It must be very hard."

Sopi sighed. "He was the last. The last of fifteen."

In the Beng language, nothing else sounded like the term for fifteen—*bu a sing song*, ten plus five. Still, I hoped I misheard.

"May god let you out of it," I murmured.

"*Auuuung*," Sopi responded mechanically. "I'll tell you about the other fourteen." And she proceeded to narrate the saddest birth history I'd ever heard. Of her fifteen children, all but one had died as babies or toddlers. Indeed, Sopi rarely had more than two children living at the same time—often, one died while she was pregnant with the next. Each time Sopi told of another child dying, she clapped her hands and then opened them with an empty gesture—a sign the Beng use to denote the concept of zero, nothing.

The closest I'd come to experiencing such a tragedy was in my sixth month of pregnancy with Nathaniel when my mother called, sobbing that she'd just been diagnosed with lung cancer. For the remaining three months I worried that my mother might never live to see her first grandchild. Thankfully, she survived the grueling rounds of chemotherapy and eventually the cancer, but the troubling memory of that time laced with fear remained vivid. The thought of attending my own child's funeral while carrying another was too painful to contemplate. I looked over at Nathaniel, who played with Bapu nearby, fashioning some sort of chair out of sticks. These days Philip and I kept our son under close watch, since Matatu had escaped his confinement and run away. He could be anywhere. Too often, I thought I saw him lurking in the corner of my vision. Gone were the days when Nathaniel could run about the village freely with his friends.

Sopi kept insisting that the same disease killed all fourteen of her children. "The disease isn't that rare. We call it blé kinlé. On both sides of the rib cage, there's a depression right under the breastbone. That's where the disease lives. Sometimes at night when my babies slept, I saw those depressions move up and down under the sheet. Many children come down with it at the same time—usually during the dry season, when it's very dusty."

The old woman continued her saga. "Only my second child escaped the terrible illness and survived childhood." Sopi dabbed her eyes with her small square of bark cloth. Meant for a mourner to absorb the inevitable tears of grief, Sopi's bark cloth appeared as soft as cotton.

She continued, "My son grew up, married, and became a father. But a few months before you and Kouadio arrived in the village, he got sick. He went to the hospital; the doctor said he had yellow fever. He recovered a bit and returned to the village to work on his farm—it was the season for clearing the yam fields, and he had a lot of work to do. But then he fell sick again. One of his sons took him to a hospital in Bouaké. The doctors thought he was cured, but the evening he was supposed to leave the city, he developed a fever and died that night. His body was brought back to the village for burial. Yellow fever killed him." She paused, anticipating my next question. "He hadn't gotten a shot to protect against it."

Straining to imagine the depths of Sopi's heartache, I had no words to say.

Amenan filled in the weight of the silence. "Children with the disease that caught Sopi's babies can be cured if the disease hasn't been caused by witchcraft. We have some good herb medicines for it."

Sopi insisted, "There *was* witchcraft involved: *jánì*—there's the reason! Me, I've been called a witch—but never, never!"

"Grandmother," I asked timidly, "who was responsible for the witchcraft?"

She replied, "My mother tried to find out. A diviner told her to offer sacrifices, and she offered palm wine, she gave *sraka* sacrifices of food to the children of the village, she sacrificed sheep, she begged the witches to release my children. We never found out who they were, but I do know who killed my son who just died. She's a young woman in my matriclan. It's hard for a witch so young to kill someone much older. But this young woman confessed."

I must have betrayed a skeptical look.

"It's true," Sopi insisted. "She's notorious. If children spend time with her in the fields, after returning to the village they all come down with fevers."

Amenan agreed. "You know the elder who's ailing now? She made him sick, too."

I wished I could interview this young woman, but surely she'd protest these accusations vigorously—just as Sopi had done. Everyone always seemed willing to ascribe witchcraft to someone else, rarely to confess. I reminded myself that I wasn't in Africa as a lawyer, trying to get to the bottom of who was responsible for any deaths ascribed to witchcraft. Or maybe there wasn't a bottom—maybe it was just a game of mystical musical chairs.

☰ I sat at the desk in the compound, calculating from Dieudonné's time sheets the average number of people who typically held a baby in a given hour. They were passed around even more than I'd expected—sometimes as often as every five minutes.

I looked up as Maat, André's second wife, approached to greet me. The ritual exchanges complete, Maat pulled over a chair while I punched in the last numbers on my calculator. Finally she lowered her voice and said in French, "Alise, my co-wife's daughter, wants to speak with you."

I nodded.

"It's about Alise's aunt. She's a member of a powerful cult," Maat near-whispered. "There are only four women in it from each village at any given time."

"Go on," I urged Maat quietly.

"Alise's aunt has recently joined the cult. To become a full member, she has to bewitch a woman from her clan during childbirth."

Maat paused to let the gravity of this news sink in. "In our village, the women of this cult conduct all the rituals for new widows and widowers," she explained. "In Kosangbé, they also do the *fewa* funeral rituals for parents who have just lost their first child."

I remembered well being chased away from a secret *fewa* ritual years ago in that village. "So, is Alise pregnant . . ." I started.

"No," Maat interrupted, "but she almost died in childbirth last year. Her aunt bewitched her, and the baby's umbilical cord came out at the same time as the body. The only reason Alise didn't die is that her aunt was in the fields at the time and distracted. Now Alise is scared to get pregnant again—until her aunt kills someone else in the clan while she's in labor. After that, her aunt won't have to bewitch anyone else, and Alise will be safe."

"I see . . ." I said, though I still wasn't sure why Maat, who, like her husband André, was a Catholic, told me this chilling story.

"So Alise would like advice about birth control right now. She's ready to speak to you tonight."

"Yes, of course," I said, stunned.

Early in the summer, I told Amenan that I'd brought several hundred condoms to make available to village residents, but when I opened up a package and explained to her how a condom worked, my friend disappointed me. She just shook her head, giggling.

"Our men will never accept that!" she declared. "If you hold a meeting about these things, people won't even talk to you any more. Better let me start circulating word quietly among the women. We'll see if anyone's interested. But I doubt it."

Amenan was right. That box of supplies sat untouched in the corner of our hut. Now, perhaps, they would find some use—if for reasons I'd never imagined.

☰ The sun had long set. We were only three days past the new moon, and the courtyard was barely lit when Maat appeared at the edge of the compound, followed by Alise, who glanced about her, worried that someone might see her. Without a word, the two women moved into the protective darkness of some nearby coffee trees, and I followed. Amenan discreetly stayed away.

We whispered the formal greetings, and I stared at Alise's pretty face. She was just a child when Philip and I first stayed in her father André's compound; now she was a young woman asking me to help protect her from witchcraft.

I began to show Alise a sample from the box, but she sighed and interrupted. "My husband would never agree to condoms. Is there something else, something I could hide from him?"

I went through the practicalities in my mind: the Pill, an IUD, and a contraceptive patch were all out of reach for a village woman. By my reckoning, Alise had only one option: the rhythm method.

I explained the method to Maat in French, who translated my words into Beng for Alise. I thought this mediated speech might embarrass Alise less than if I spoke in Beng, but once we got down to the technicalities she dove right in. "So how do I know when the egg is there?" she asked.

I explained how to calculate the seven infertile days of the cycle before ovulation.

"And then I can't have sex after that for how many days?"

"For the next twelve days. Then you can have sex until you get your period."

She nodded.

Now it was my turn to ask a question. "How will you keep track of the days?"

Alise thought for a moment, then said, "I'll make a mark with charcoal on a piece of bark cloth for every day, starting when I get my period."

"Good idea. This method isn't perfect, but it works best if you keep careful track of the days."

We rehearsed the schedule details once more, then she and Maat slunk off to the other side of the village under cover of night. Participating in this subversive rebellion felt a bit exciting—but I didn't like the implication that a woman who practices birth control has something to be ashamed of, especially if she thinks she's saving her life.

Hard as it was to imagine at that moment, in less than two weeks I'd be teaching an Introduction to Anthropology class. Alise's story might give my students an expanded sense of how modern birth-control techniques are accepted or rejected in places far from America. But my students might find it too easy to dismiss her as yet another "superstitious" African, too easy to mock her temporary efforts at birth control, limned as they were by fear of witchcraft. Would I be able to convey the dignity of Alise's earnest efforts to find a way out of danger?

PHILIP: GIFTING PARTY

We arrived in Kosangbé with a full car: in the trunk lay the stereo system we were delivering to the village, and in the back beside Nathaniel sat Bertin and Augustin, who had come to help with any technical kinks. I parked on the side of the dirt road that divided Kosangbé, near stacks of blue plastic chairs that had been delivered to the village yesterday.

No one had touched them, which surprised me. The elders were surely itching to settle into them, to finally, like the elders in other, more prosperous villages, feel the respect built into the chairs' comfortable plastic curves. This must mean that the Kosangbé elders had a presentation ceremony planned, and we'd be listening to a lot of speeches. How could I have forgotten that? Certainly Nathaniel hadn't, peering out the window in the back seat—accustomed to the long rituals of Beng speechifying, he'd brought along one of those Jo and Zette books by Hergé we'd discovered in Abidjan.

The village children ran to us, surrounding Bertin and Augustin as they lifted the stereo components from the trunk. "*Ka ta!*"—Go away!—Augustin shouted, but they merely giggled and took a few steps back. Nathaniel kept close beside the two college students, a quiet declaration that he was one of the experts too, and they marched the speakers under the palm-leaf veranda of the men's meeting place. The elders approached from the other side of the village: the chief, San Kofi; his older brother and our former nemesis, San Yao, who, in a light blue *bubu*, looked even frailer than he had earlier this summer; and Ché Kofi, the speaker for all those coming speeches.

Yacouba arrived, and I tried to match his hearty welcome, even though this would be one of our last times together before we left for home. I wondered if his beaming face masked the same sad thought. After our greetings Alma and I asked him if some of those chairs could finally be unstacked and set out for the elders. Yacouba nodded, and soon a semicircle of the most modern Ivorian chairs stood beside a line of spare parts for the village's repaired water pump, on temporary display for the ceremony to come. Yes indeed, a lot of speeches were in the cards.

As the elders settled, I kept scanning the crowd of villagers: so many children I didn't recognize, who had been born since our previous stays, many of them now nearly teenagers, and so many teenagers from those days who were now adults. Mainly, though, I searched for a glimpse of Matatu, who hadn't yet been caught. I kept alert because this was just the sort of gathering where the Big Man might appear, unwanted. Though maybe he wouldn't dare, afraid of capture. Maybe he was hiding, miles away, far from any Beng village, that prime minister inside him biding his time.

First San Kofi spoke in low tones to Ché Kofi, then to San Yao, and after he repeated their words louder for our benefit, Yacouba murmured a French translation for whatever we missed. As the speeches continued, I noticed that Alma didn't take notes, wasn't holding a notebook at all. Had she left it in the car when we arrived? I considered alerting her, but held back at the sight of her misty-eyed smile, the sign that my wife is especially pleased or moved. While this was an important anthropological moment, I guessed for Alma it was trumped by the personal. For years following our first time among the Beng, she had regretted her decision to live in Kosangbé. The villagers' suspicions had taken so long to ease that she came to believe she never should have imposed herself. I had certainly criticized her healthy stubborn streak. Yet now the elders, sitting on those blue plastic chairs, offered speeches that made it clear they were glad we had lived among them. Whatever my wife might lose by not writing down their words would be offset by her savoring of this emotional moment. We had come full circle, shown the Kosangbé villagers that we had managed to learn enough of Beng ways to behave honorably in their eyes, that all along we'd been deserving of their trust.

Then two young men stepped forward with a sheep, and Ché Kofi announced this was Kosangbé's gift of thanks to us. Now it was our turn for speeches and thanks, and Alma trotted out her best Beng to express our appreciation for the villagers' patience with us so long ago. Beside us, Nathaniel quietly turned the pages of Jo and Zette's adventures, too young to understand the importance of this occasion for his parents.

When we'd wrung out the last possible drop of ritual thanks, now came the time the children and young people had been waiting for—the setting up of the stereo system, to be followed by dancing. Bertin and Augustin eased the components from the boxes and untangled the wires. Nathaniel, happy that *finally* something interesting was in the works, studied Bertin coolly fiddling with the connections.

The thick electric cable we'd purchased in Abidjan now looped around the corner of a mud-brick house and continued for yards to the edge of the forest, where Augustin connected it to a hefty orange block of a gas generator. This unwieldy contraption—donated years ago by loggers in payment for permission to chop down trees near the village—would power the stereo, but it also made a terrible racket, which was why we'd picked the longest cable available, to keep the noise as far from the dance space as possible.

With everything seemingly in place, Bertin slipped a tape into the tape deck, waved to Augustin, who waved to someone out of our sight, and up rose the low roar of the generator.

No music.

"We'll have to try again," Bertin said, unplugging the stereo wires. He examined them silently, perhaps recalling his previous experience with recalcitrant stereos at college parties in the capital. Augustin joined him, and together they made a big show that this was a minor problem, easily overcome.

A bit of rewiring, another set of signals from Bertin to Augustin to the unseen villager, and again the generator rumbled alive. Again, no music.

Bertin pressed his lips together, trying to hide his concern. He and Augustin returned to huddling at the back of the stereo receiver, and now I worried that maybe the bumpy dirt-road ride from Asagbé had loosened something in the tape deck—or worse, that we'd bought the wrong components back in Abidjan.

"Non, pas ici," Bertin murmured as Augustin pointed a wire at something. Alma paced nervously, and even the elders rustled in their comfy new chairs. I wondered how much longer they would let the technologically savvy college students fuss about, before they intervened and invoked the forest spirits to get the music started.

I watched Bertin calmly assess the problem. He and Augustin had done excellent work for Alma this summer, and we worried about their futures. In response to political protests on campus this past spring, the government had shut down the university for the remainder of the school year, and canceled student scholarships. What would these two young men do once we left? Bertin—unlike Augustin—spoke English, and Alma and I had quietly begun entertaining the audacious notion that we might be able to find him a place at our own university.

Finally, another set of signals, another distant generator grumble, and this time the music started up. Cheers from the children punctuated the fizzy Ivorian guitars and percussion speeding along: this was a hit song everyone seemed to recognize, and the young men and women bobbed their heads, bodies swaying, feet lightly stamping the ground.

As the dancing continued, San Kofi—as chief, too dignified to join in—motioned to Nathaniel, then reached out and sat him on his lap. Nathaniel accepted with surprising grace, settling in as if Kofi were an old relative, and a part of me exulted in this further example of differences bridged after all these years. However, another part of me, watching the sunken-eyed and white-haired San Yao who stood beside them, couldn't quite erase my wariness about our old foe. I wondered if both versions would forever jostle inside me, or if today's San Yao would eventually win out, revising his former self.

☰   The screen door banged shut behind me as I headed to the outhouse. I paused at the sight of Kokora Kouassi's older brother Yao, who sat on a stool in the middle of the courtyard, bent over a wooden bowl resting on the ground, dripping water into it from a dark cloth, murmuring something.

"What's with Yao?" I asked Alma, who stood off to the side with Amenan, watching him.

"He's praying," she replied, her voice almost a whisper.

"Praying? Him?" I said too loud, drawing Alma's frown. "I mean," I continued, my words now a whisper, "why? What's going on?"

By this time, Yao had finished his prayer, and he glanced about, eyes unfocused, as if he'd just awakened.

"He's praying for the return of the sheep."

"Oh," I said, though still a bit confused. Two days ago as promised, Yacouba and a small delegation of young men had arrived in Amenan's compound with Kosangbé's gift of a sheep. However, the doomed creature had escaped overnight, and yesterday's many searches throughout the village had failed. So now Amenan's family were enlisting the help of spirits. Why Yao? The old man was a dour sort—I don't think I'd ever seen him smile. With one arm withered since childhood—which the Beng surely believed was caused by witchcraft—he'd lived most of his life in the wake of his spiritually powerful younger brother. I generally tried to stay out of his way.

"Didn't Aba Kouassi offer a prayer yesterday?" I asked.

"Yeah, but it doesn't seem to have worked. Amenan said everyone feels shamed for losing that sheep. It's a big deal—she confessed that her family owes the spirits a sheep for some divination performed a while ago, so now the spirits have snatched up ours instead. Amenan thinks they've turned it invisible, and that's why no one can find it. This time the oldest member of the family has to appeal to the spirits, and that's Yao."

"Hmmm," I said, continuing on my way, "good luck with that."

Returned to my desk, I'd barely settled back into a scene from my novel, set at a carnival shut down by rain, when a chorus of happy whoops and shouts rose from the forest near our compound. Now what? I thought, rising from the chair. As I stepped out, the kids playing with Nathaniel began to laugh and dance, some pointing to the edge of Amenan's coffee trees, and there marched her brother Kofi Ba, pulling the lost sheep by the rope that was still tied about its neck.

"You found him, you found him!" the children sang, and Alma grinned and said, "Can you believe it? Yao said that prayer less than an hour ago!"

I grinned back, shook my head in bemused wonder. After all my years among the Beng, I was long past trying to balance coincidence with the possibility of spiritual design. Nearby, Yao stood in a corner of the compound, quiet as usual. Something like the hint of a smile appeared on his face.

ALMA: TYING UP LOOSE ENDS

One evening after we settled Nathaniel into bed—worn out from another day of playing hard under an African sun—Philip and I returned to the courtyard and sat beside Amenan near the hearth's dying embers to revisit the day's news. We'd received word that Matatu had finally been found, wandering on foot on a dirt road some eighty kilometers away. Exhausted and compliant, he was promptly delivered to the hospital in Bouaké.

Why didn't I feel relieved?

"You know," Amenan said, "Matatu's not the only one."

Philip looked up from the mesmerizing embers. "What do you mean?"

"A few other young Beng men are crazy, too," Amenan explained. "And in just the same way Matatu is."

"Really?"

"There's another one who's even crazier than Matatu. He went to a hospital in Burkina Faso, and they cured him with some medicines. But he escaped and walked all the way back to Asagbé! When the rice ripened, he went mad again." Amenan paused. "His family has no money for another cure."

"Have we met him?" Philip asked.

"I doubt it. He lives alone in the savanna. He's not violent, though. He laughs a lot. He can speak well. And he calls himself the *premier ministre*—just like Matatu."

"*Mon dieu!*"

"There's a couple more, in some other villages. They all say they're the prime minister," Amenan said, "and they threaten to condemn you to death if you insult them. Strange, isn't it?"

Philip and I had long suspected that Matatu's creative delusions of grandeur, his collection of Western wealth fashioned from cast-off scraps, somehow meant more than the tragedy of one young man whose life had gone awry. Now, learning that Matatu was not alone in his symptoms, I wondered if his disturbing fantasies were a strange but almost reasonable statement of despair. In recent years, the nation's once-promising future seemed in danger of vanishing, and Matatu had joined his fellow prime ministers in imagined power rather than face the near certainty of lifelong poverty.

Philip seemed to have read my mind as he turned to me. "When I think of how we showed up with all this *stuff*—cameras, typewriters, even a car for god's sake. Every day, we pushed in his face how poor he is and always will be. We're lucky we haven't driven anyone else nuts."

Biting my lip, I thought back to the healer's explanation of Matatu's madness as caused by witchcraft in his family. Our neighbors accepted this interpretation, but the anthropologist in me felt impelled to ask more questions. Amenan's announcement that many more would-be prime ministers roamed the Beng landscape underlined for me the troubling territory between madness and the modern in Matatu's precariously balanced inner life.

In the silence following Amenan's revelation, I became aware of a child tearfully protesting a late-night bath in a neighboring compound, then the crackling of the hearth's dying fire. I rested my spiral notebook on my lap, turned on the flashlight I always kept with me in the dark, clicked open my pen, and began to write.

≋ We sat on stools across from Bertin and his parents in their courtyard, and Bertin's many younger siblings congregated in quiet excitement around our small circle. They had no idea what was occurring, but they could tell it must be something worth watching.

This Kosangbé compound we'd lived next to fourteen years ago hadn't changed much, but our mission today couldn't be more different. Far from settling in to learn about religious practices in this most fiercely traditional of all Beng villages, we now assembled around the hearth of François and Makola, our former hosts, to suggest a momentous change for their family's future.

Philip opened with the first of what would be many ritualized speeches, with Yacouba serving as our formal speaker. "François, you yourself went to school for a few years, and you know how valuable it was. That's why you decided to send Bertin to first grade."

Despite being the center of discussion, Bertin—following Beng etiquette—remained silent as Yacouba repeated Philip's words.

François nodded.

"Bertin was the first child from the village to complete elementary school," Philip continued, "and look how far he's gone."

"*Ah-heh*," François intoned. When François had enrolled his son in the Sangbé school three miles down the road, he had sent his oldest son on a one-way street out of the village, as Bertin had continued on to junior high in the town of M'Bahiakro, then high school in Béoumi, and then the National University of Côte d'Ivoire in Abidjan.

"But now that scholarships are canceled, Bertin can't pay the fees next year," I added. "And even if he could, what if there's another strike? It's likely he won't complete his degree."

"*Oui, oui*," François said.

"We've discussed the situation with Bertin. We'd like to try to help him transfer to our university in America."

"Mm-hmm," came François' noncommittal response.

I glanced across at Bertin, a study in self-control. His impassive face betrayed no strong emotion, yet he must have ached to jump into this conversation about his future. Although in his midtwenties, Bertin wasn't married, so he remained a child in Beng law. Not only did he lack the right to leave his homeland without his parents' permission, Beng etiquette didn't allow him to make the request.

"With an American degree," I continued through Yacouba, "when Bertin returns to Côte d'Ivoire, he can put his new skills to work to help the whole village, even the whole Beng area. That's what Busu is doing . . ."

François nodded.

A distant uncle of Bertin's on his mother's side, Busu had traveled to Canada some years ago to complete a master's degree, then returned to take up a government position as a port inspector, and Busu had shared his good fortune not only with his extended family but with his natal village of Manigbé. The story of Busu's success had helped Philip and me envision a different way to thank the Beng. It was one thing to offer material gifts to our two villages. But some day, the mill would break down, the blue plastic chairs would collapse, the water pump's spare parts would wear out. When we had initially spoken with Bertin about sponsoring him as a student at our university, he had readily understood the weight that would be on his shoulders by accepting this offer.

Bertin's mother Makola shifted on her stool. "He'll be very far from his family," she pointed out. "He's already traveled so far from the village, ever since he was six . . ." A dignified woman from a royal line, Makola often intimidated me with her composure; I'd never heard her voice trail off in sadness.

I judged this the moment to offer the promise that Philip and I had agreed to. "If he comes to America with us," I said, "Kouadio and I will serve in your place, as Bertin's father and mother, and N'zri Denju will be his little brother. We'll make sure he has enough food to eat. If he gets sick, we'll take him to a doctor. If he makes any mistakes, we'll correct him. If he gets into any trouble, we'll help him get out of it."

Satisfied, François rose to shake our hands. "May god keep him healthy, and may god give you all you ask for. We put our trust in you."

We gave thanks to each other, and François brought out a *bidon* of palm wine to offer a prayer to the ancestors. As we passed around a hollowed-out gourd to share drinks, I couldn't help worrying about this pact we'd made, couldn't help worrying if Philip and I would be able to fulfill the many promises we'd made.

We continued making the round of good-byes from one courtyard to the next, first stopping at San Kofi's to thank the village for the gift of the sheep. We left Yacouba's compound for last. No matter how many years claimed us between visits, our friendship always seemed to pick up where we left off, yet I dreaded the sad farewells we were about to exchange today, and hoped that this latest separation wouldn't last too long.

≋ Kofi half-roused assorted sleeping children in the compound and carried them in for the night while Evelyne finished washing the dinner dishes. Earlier in the day, Evelyne and her husband, Kwamela, who was visiting from M'Bahiakro, had asked me about the cache of condoms that Philip and I had brought to Bengland—apparently, she'd gotten word of them from Amenan, and she was interested. Kwamela, who made a good living as a tailor, had said something I never thought I'd hear a Beng man say: "We want a family, but not so many children that we can't afford to send them to school." Evelyne would return to live with her husband at the end of the summer; at least some village ways were losing their grip on this young couple.

The courtyard was quiet now, yet still I lingered outside at our table, our kerosene lantern casting just enough dim light to illuminate my notebook's jottings. I was on the lookout for one more question to ask, one more connection to pull everything together, explain the Beng world to me once and for all. Tying up loose ends always feels like a doomed exercise in frustration for an anthropologist. But who knew when we'd return?

The statistical charts that Dieudonné had filled in, chronicling how the babies he'd observed spent their time, along with all my scores of transcribed interviews with mothers, brought me a certain peace of mind that I had enough data to write a book about Beng babies' lives. Emerging from an afterlife as rich as any imagined place of the spirit, these babies were greeted by a world of relatives who spared no effort to lure their newborns into this life—through nearly constant breastfeeding day and night by mothers, who also bejeweled and painted their children's tiny bodies twice daily; and constant carrying, talking, singing, and playing with an extended family's many children and adults. But all this communal coddling would amount to nothing if their mothers' breasts ran dry from poverty. The book I'd write about Beng babies would need to shed one bright light on the spiritual and emotional wealth of their young lives, another on the dark challenge of their poverty.

Amenan finished sweeping the last corner of the courtyard and approached to rest on a stool near me. "I can't believe it's almost time for us to leave," I forced myself to say. That evening we'd offered our formal thanks and farewells to Kokora Kouassi. Filled with gratitude for the kindness of our old friend's dreams about my family this summer, I watched him, frail and nearly blind, begin a prayer for our safe journey. I knew Aba Kouassi worried about the future—he hadn't yet identified a successor to his position as Asagbé's Master of the Earth. So many young men in the village were converting to Islam or Christianity, who would continue his spiritual legacy? Philip and I had shared glances of regret, afraid we might never see him again.

Now Amenan quietly pressed me for a return date. I hesitated. Philip and I were hoping to have a second child in the next year or so, and new family responsibilities would certainly push a return to Bengland farther back than my friend would like. But how could I speak of this? The ancestral warning of a countless line of Jewish grandmothers not to tempt the fates and talk of something that hasn't yet happened—"Don't give yourself a *kinehura*"—kept me silent. I, too, had my own mystical fears.

Instead I asked her to estimate the cost of building a new two-room house for our next stay. She said she'd discuss it with some relatives, and we both fell silent. How could we leave, I thought, when the Beng world still held me? Tahan's curse of her sister Evelyne's approaching delivery hadn't gone to trial yet, while across the village Alise feared the consequences of a new pregnancy. And how long might Kofi stay in Asagbé before disappearing again? Anthropologists always leave in the middle, I thought ruefully.

Finally I said, "You know, there's something I've wanted to ask you ever since our first day back in the village."

Amenan looked at me, surprised. I forged on. "Why has your mother been so sad all summer?"

Amenan released a lengthy sigh and hunched down on her stool. After fourteen years of friendship, I always knew when I was in for a long story. Amenan then recounted a recent hidden wound at the center of her mother's life—a domestic drama that had rendered the formerly vibrant woman nearly immobile and mute. It pained me to contemplate this family saga—now as clear to me as it had been invisible until moments before. How could I ever write about it? The temptation of the anthropologist to tell all felt too invasive here; I had plenty of other lives to narrate.

I closed my notebook, lifted the lantern from the table. This story would not be told, this loose end would brook no tying up.

PHILIP: SHOOTING FISH

We walked through the center of Grand Bassam, its buildings as dilapidated as when I'd stayed here briefly during the Ivorian literary conference three years ago. The town once served as the colonial capital of Côte d'Ivoire but now mainly survived as a run-down attraction for tourists. Considering the country's history, I found it easy to resist nostalgia for any departed splendor. Beside us walked Hank Drewal, an art historian we met in Abidjan who'd also been doing research this summer in Côte d'Ivoire. Hank pointed out some of his favorite details, like a set of stone steps leading up to the second floor of an empty building, as we passed one deserted colonial government building and mansion after another, overgrown with vines and smeared with wide swaths of tropical mold. Local women strolled past these relics with impossibly heavy loads on their heads, the slow sashay of their daily lives' hard work.

Why this neglect? There were surely more than a handful of corrupt Ivorian officials who had diverted enough wealth their way to be able to restore this classic architecture of another time into ostentatious summer homes. I thought of the millions upon millions that President Houphouët-Boigny had spent on his personal cathedral while the monuments in this town languished. Unless neglect was the point, letting time take its slow revenge. Maybe these buildings' route nearly to the edge of ruins felt right, somehow, to modern Ivorians, a satisfying example of the end of the colonial era, with its legacy of resource robbing and forced labor. This was lovingly attended decay.

After a turn about the town, we settled at a *maquis* near the beach for a seafood lunch. As we divided up the portions of a sizable whole fish, Hank pointed out on the wall behind us a local artist's painting of Mami Wata, the mermaid-like goddess worshipped throughout West Africa and across the ocean in Brazil. Framed by thick dark hair, her brown face seemed possessed as she stared forward, a serpent coiling across her shoulders. She was a complicated goddess who ruled the waters, seductive and scary, able to make your fortune or twist your fate.

I looked down at my plate, the delicate white meat of a fish lying on a bed of *attiéké* and a sleek sauce of onions and tomatoes. Perhaps a creature from the sea wasn't the best meal to enjoy beneath her stare.

After lunch, we parted company with Hank and headed back to Abidjan on the main road that ran parallel to the coast, catching glimpses through the palm trees of the restless edge of the Atlantic Ocean and the occasional tiny village of thatch-roofed mud-brick huts. These must be the homes of the fishers who provided food for the restaurants of Grand Bassam, brave souls who very likely kept private shrines to Mami Wata, in the hopes that she would watch over them in the open sea.

I would miss Africa's tight weave of invisible powers and unseen presences. In two days, we'd fly home to the United States, but I could imagine my father's spirit staying behind: he'd always wanted to travel and now, belatedly, here was his chance to become a kind of anthropologist in the afterlife. Kokora Kouassi's dreams had given me more of a gift than I'd first suspected: *wurugbé* was now an alternate space where I could keep the memory of my father, far away from the past, from my difficult childhood. And if his ghost did remain in Bengland, then the culture's cosmology had worked out a rough exchange, inspiring within me a collection of fictional ghosts when I'd mourned my father back in the village. In the coming years I'd be further imagining them, slowly shaping their developing paths on the page.

Sitting in the back seat and constructing something with his remaining Legos, Nathaniel barely noticed the ocean beach outside our car windows. How much, I wondered, had settled into him this summer? When we'd slaughtered the sheep that Kosangbé had given us, Nathaniel had watched intently, undisturbed by the spectacle of a living creature being meticulously transformed into the various parts of a future stew. He fit right in, much the same way he'd casually picked up a machete to clear away brush on the edge of Amenan's compound. What would he remember later in his life from this summer? Perhaps some busy jumble of Tintin's escapades and Matatu's magic bag, an offstage ancestor's borrowed name, his village pals, the bitterness of his weekly antimalaria pill, a seismograph especially tailored for a vicious little *piste*, a dying infant, a generous food fairy, the long trail of a car's alarm, and his grandfather's village funeral. What, I wondered, would dig down deep inside him, only to appear later in ways that couldn't easily be translated?

Soon enough we drew closer to Abidjan and passed the airport, then came to the familiar busy roundabout, and I slowed to negotiate the curving traffic until a gendarme flagged me to a stop.

"Oh no," Alma groaned.

I took my papers from the glove compartment as he sauntered over, wearing creepy reflector sunglasses that hid his gaze.

"*Pardon, monsieur*, but you shouldn't drive so fast," he tisked.

Speeding, are you kidding? I wanted to say but didn't. Instead, I offered him the car registration, and took my driver's license from my wallet.

"No, no," he waved them away. "Your passports."

When we produced them, he slipped all three into a shirt pocket. "I'll have to keep these, until the court hearing."

"A court hearing? When will that be?" I asked, stunned.

"Oh, in two or three weeks," he replied, his voice thick with boredom, ready, apparently, to dismiss us.

"Two or three—but we have a plane flight in two days, we—"

The shock of this last-minute disaster dissolved when I noticed, behind his mocking smile, three other gendarmes who had flagged down cars in the roundabout. He and his buddies were shooting fish in a barrel, flagrantly snagging one easy bribe after another from whites, Ivorians, whoever drove a halfway decent car. There would be no court appearance, only an exchange of valuables: our passports for cash. I still held my wallet in my hand, so I eased out the edge of a banknote and waited. He showed no emotion, so I eased out another. He nodded, just barely, and within seconds our passports magically reappeared.

"*Merci*," I muttered, instantly flushed with anger at myself for thanking him, and I drove off.

Over the years I'd grown used to gendarmes' furtive shakedowns, but this one seemed especially blatant, since these guys didn't even appear concerned who might be watching as they so openly went about their extracurricular business. Oh, calm down, I thought, it's just a bribe, a little nothing in the annals of Ivorian corruption. Yet something about that incident nagged at me, as if the pressure of the country's economic troubles had begun to loosen unspoken constraints.

A Different Fieldwork Site

JANUARY 1994

ALMA: CONVERGING PATHS

In the front seat, Philip clutched the wheel and kept eerily silent, fiddling now and then with the dashboard dials to try and coax another degree out of our station wagon's heater. In the back seat, Nathaniel and I huddled together as close as our seat belts allowed, adjusting a blanket to keep warm.

The radio's weather report periodically warned us that it was 21 below zero outside, nearly minus 60 with the wind chill—one of the coldest days in the history of Illinois. I didn't need this grim statistic to be repeated, I already had it memorized, even though we'd just begun our 135-mile trek north to O'Hare Airport. There, Bertin Kouadio would be arriving in a few hours from Côte d'Ivoire. It seemed insane to drive in such weather, but we couldn't abandon Bertin in the airport.

The time and miles passed slowly as we drove through long stretches of farmland—what would transform into lush fields of corn and soybeans come summer, now resembled the last traces of a dying planet, with dried-out corn stubble covered in bitter frost. Occasionally we'd pass a car that had been abandoned along the snowy shoulder of the highway and I'd exchange a glance with Philip in the rearview mirror, but we said nothing, not wanting to alarm Nathaniel, who sat curled into a book. The opening week of first grade, soon after we returned from Côte d'Ivoire, he'd been tested at a third-grade reading level. Surprised, we'd asked Nathaniel how he'd learned to read so well.

"When Daddy was reading the Tintin books to me," he'd explained, "I followed along."

"But why didn't you tell us you could read?" Philip had asked.

"I was afraid if you knew, you'd stop reading to me."

Now I looked at my son turning pages and decided I'd offer to read to him later. At the moment my mind was elsewhere. What might Bertin be thinking, on the long hours of his first international flight? By this time, the plane must have crossed over the Atlantic coast of the United States, just as we sped north to Chicago. Soon our paths, and lives, would converge at O'Hare Airport.

Last fall, Bertin had worked so hard and so well on the remaining stages of the government grant for the Asagbé mill that even the new American ambassador had been impressed, and wrote a letter in support of his visa application. Bertin left Côte d'Ivoire just in time, I thought. The long-ailing Houphouët-Boigny had finally died last month, and because he hadn't established a clear line of succession, I didn't have high hopes for the country's continued stability.

Still, I worried. Bertin's university grades back in Abidjan were fine, and he spoke English well enough, but he hadn't yet passed a demanding language-proficiency test at a level high enough to satisfy our campus. We'd already signed him up for an intensive English-for-foreign-students course, and we hoped eight hours of classes five days a week would get his skills up to speed. After all, besides Beng, he knew four other African languages, and French was his sixth language. Now he'd have to further master a seventh. In the meantime, he'd be living in the spare bedroom of our house, becoming a member of our small family. Nathaniel would suddenly have a much older brother, and Philip and I would take on the role of parents of a college student. What were we getting ourselves into?

"It's the coldest day in the history of—"

"Could you please turn that down?" I asked Philip.

"Okay, but just a little. I need to keep track of the weather."

I looked out the window at the endless flat fields until they nearly hypnotized me and wondered what Bertin would make of this wintry lunar landscape. Who could have predicted he'd arrive on a day that broke cold-weather records? I had no illusions that the down jacket, the hat and gloves we'd brought along for him would provide anything near the warmth he felt accustomed to, after having spent all his life in the tropics.

I'd long imagined what it might be like to host my friend Amenan in America, to watch her express incomprehension and shock, ask naïve question after question until even I tired of answering them. But Bertin was a city boy. Still, many sights in America would be new for him—

"Look, there's the exit for O'Hare," Philip announced. Soon Bertin would begin his first day in a foreign country, negotiating everything in English, on the coldest day of his life.

I had thought, after picking up Bertin at the airport, that a short detour through downtown Chicago might be a good idea before the long haul through the prairie to our home in Urbana. The city might remind him of Abidjan and could offer a welcome urban view before we drove for over a hundred miles through a bleak Illinois farmscape. But the deep freeze kept nearly everyone indoors, and we drove through an eerily deserted city, the glass-walled skyscrapers looking like enormous frozen stalagmites. Chicago might as well have been a ghost town. "Look, the Water Tower . . . look, the Art Institute . . . look, the Field Museum," Alma kept helpfully pointing out. Bertin merely nodded, staring with alarm at the sight of his own breath rising in the air like a tiny cloud.

Soon we returned to the highway, and I drove as fast as I dared, anxious to reach home before darkness fell. Alma read a book to Nathaniel in the back seat, Bertin sat lost in his thoughts beside me, and I concentrated on the road—though I had to admit to a mean-spirited satisfaction competing with my empathy. Even after all these years, the shock of our first arrival in Bengland sometimes still felt raw to me, and now here was a Beng person enduring a similar shock, on our home turf.

And like us, Bertin was arriving with far more than he could ever fit in a suitcase. I remembered him telling me back in Asagbé that he was convinced Matatu had been bewitched. Yes, Bertin was a university student, but that didn't prevent him from believing in the invisible powers his culture recognized. Ah well, I thought, Nathaniel had brought his own sense of African spirituality back home. Once, after losing my temper when he argued about clearing the dinner table—one of his household chores—Nathaniel left the room insulted and hurt. Feeling remorse for my sharp words, my loud voice—too loud, I was often told—I followed him to the kitchen, where he sat in a corner, chin resting on his knees, glowering. I leaned in to apologize, but before I could he hissed, "You, you came *dangerously close* to having to sacrifice a sheep." My surprised laughter didn't improve our possible reconciliation, but I couldn't help myself—I'd forgotten that my son was also N'zri Denju, reincarnated ancestor who deserved special deference. Clearly Nathaniel hadn't forgotten.

Frost kept forming on the side windows from our breath, which Alma did her best to scrape off. Our car seemed to be slowly turning into a mobile ice cave, and I worried that the car engine might lock up from the cold. We should have stayed in Chicago, I thought, rented a couple of hotel rooms.

Bertin slumped deeper and deeper into the passenger seat beside me, as if pressed down by the view outside: endless flat fields laced with snow and drifts, out of which poked the remains of last summer's dead corn stalks, with a farm house, a silo off in the distance, framed against a relentless gray sky. Surely this landscape corresponded to no picture Bertin had ever seen or imagined of the United States. He must have been misinformed—America was actually a sort of frozen hell, a trap for unsuspecting Africans foolish enough to travel here in hopes of a better life . . .

"Don't go outside," the radio announcer reminded us, "it's so cold you could freeze to death in less than ten minutes." This warning certainly frightened me, why shouldn't it alarm Bertin?

I raised my voice over the radio so he could hear me instead. "Don't worry, this all looks much better in the summer, when everything is growing. It's just farmland. Our town is much, much nicer. And the university is beautiful."

He stared at me, barely nodding. I could be part of the plot, after all.

≋   Alma and Nathaniel showed Bertin the guest room upstairs while I busied myself in the kitchen. The night before, I'd prepared a West African–inspired stew of chicken in peanut sauce, to remind him of home. All I had to do was reheat it while cooking some rice, and we'd have our first meal as an expanded family.

Bertin sat quietly during dinner, eating little, and saying less, haltingly. Though English had been his best subject in school, the spoken American version was giving him trouble. After polite but subdued thanks, he returned to his room.

As I cleaned up in the kitchen with Alma, I remembered that tonight, at the nearby indoor sports stadium on campus, a monster truck rally would soon crank up. I'd never been to one myself, though I'd seen enough of the commercials for the show: ordinary pickup trucks with wheels larger than a person, pulling wheelies in the air and smashing down on a row of junker cars; motorcyclists' high-speed gymnastics in the air; a dinosaur-sized mechanical monster breathing fire, clutching a car with giant claws and tearing it apart with metal teeth; and all accompanied by the PA system's frenetic competition between an announcer's drill-sergeant growl of a voice and dizzy heavy-metal guitar arpeggios. Maybe Bertin could use some distraction from the worries that must be overwhelming him.

Alma didn't agree.

"You want to *what*?" she asked.

"Go to the monster truck rally. C'mon, what could be a better introduction to American culture?"

"You mean the *worst* introduction, don't you?"

"Not at all. Look, it only comes to town once a ye—"

"You're joking, right?"

"No, it'll be—"

"Horrible. Bertin's already in shock, or hadn't you noticed?"

I had. Yet something inside me wanted to put Bertin through the ringer, to test his limits the way his culture had tested mine. Alma would never allow this, and I felt secretly relieved by her opposition. At least I'd been able to express the impulse, at least I could imagine, as I wiped down the counters, Bertin's astonished face at a mechanical monster—wasn't it called Robosaur?—that chewed a car to death and belched fire at the cheering stadium.

In the morning Bertin ventured downstairs, still tired after what must have been a troubled night. Alma had made a stack of pancakes and fresh-squeezed orange juice, welcoming American comfort food for a cold morning, but I worried that Bertin might prefer a breakfast more like home: perhaps a buttered slice of baguette dipped in coffee thick with sweetened, condensed milk.

While Alma and Nathaniel set the table, Bertin stood at the living room window and stared out at the snow-covered landscape, which confirmed that yesterday's long drive hadn't been a horrible dream. I tried to imagine the scene through his eyes, recalling my first response—quiet, but stunned—to the relentless dust and mud of a Beng village; the curious crowds that hemmed us in, speaking in a language I'd somehow have to learn; the freely wandering animals; the dispiriting poverty; and I had thought, How would we manage to live here?

"Kouadio!"

Bertin leaned close to the window.

"What?" I asked, concerned by the fear in his voice.

"Outside, look!" and he pointed to two children across the street.

Two neighborhood kids were goofing around, working up a ball of snow for the bottom half of a snowman. I didn't see anything unusual.

"Do you mean those two boys?"

"Yes, in the snow! Are they in . . ."

Bertin hesitated, struggling to find the word, and I would have supplied it if I knew what he searched for. How often had a Beng word or phrase eluded me over the years! I could feel the despairing edge of Bertin's frustration as he repeated, "Are they, are they in . . . danger?"

"Danger? No, they're just playing, they're not near the street—"

"But the snow, can it . . . hurt them?"

I resisted the impulse to chuckle, thinking how much those weather reports must have affected Bertin, and I replied as reassuringly as possible. "No, it's warmer today, and kids in our country love to play in the snow. They're happy there's no school, and their mothers bundled them up before letting them outside."

Bertin nodded, not quite convinced. What kind of people are these, he per-haps wondered, whom he would have to live among? Watching him stare out the window, as if on the alert in case one of the boys fell over from the power of the fearsome snow, I realized that our living room, our entire house, our neighborhood, and beyond had become a fieldwork site. So much lay ahead for Bertin. Embarking on his own anthropological journey, he would be changed in unpredictable ways.

"Breakfast is ready!" Alma called.

We sat together in the dining room, an American couple and their son, each altered within by Africa, and joined at the table by an African young man. Bertin stared carefully at the stack of pancakes and glasses of orange juice, the strips of turkey bacon, the scrambled eggs, and I thought of how odd this must seem to him, remembered my own unease when Alma and I ate our first Beng meal and regarded the smooth white yams nestled in plates, the separate bowls filled with a green slick sauce, the men sitting on low stools in a circle by themselves, the women sitting apart with the children. Alma and I had no idea what to do next, and so we'd watched everyone else, then plucked with our fingers a bit from the oval ball of stretchy yam, dipped it in the sauce, and ate, while gamely pretending the sauce wasn't spicier than anything we'd ever eaten before in our lives. Almost no one spoke while eating.

Now, Alma announced in Beng' "*Ka'na poblé*"—Let's eat—and we passed plates back and forth across the table. Nathaniel lobbied for a sledding jaunt for later in the day, and Alma kept asking Bertin, "Is it good, do you like the food?" He nodded, eating slowly, testing these new flavors and textures, try-ing to follow the quick back and forth of our conversations and certainly unprepared—and who ever is?—for the transformations awaiting him.

Epilogue

CÔTE D'IVOIRE AND THE BENG IN CRISIS

In the final months of writing *Braided Worlds*, we remained transfixed by the news reports of the disastrous aftermath of the 2010 presidential election in Côte d'Ivoire. Though Alassane Ouattara was almost universally recognized by the world as the winner of the election, incumbent president Laurent Gbagbo, the loser, refused to concede, and in doing so plunged the country into months of economic disaster and then civil war. While we wrote about the lives of poor villagers in a remote area of Côte d'Ivoire, we watched scenes of carnage and violence in the economic capital, Abidjan, and once more we feared for the well-being of the Beng people, whose lives were affected by events beyond their control. Though as of this writing Ouattara had been forced to defeat his rival again, this time militarily, and has now been inaugurated as president, the rebuilding of the country is fraught with daunting challenges.

Côte d'Ivoire's present-day dilemma was long in coming. After helping his country win independence from France back in 1960, Houphouët-Boigny began his presidency as one of the continent's liberation heroes. And for twenty years, journalists touted Côte d'Ivoire as the West African miracle: least interethnic strife; most stable government since independence; an annual economic growth rate of nearly 8 percent; the center of manufacturing and diplomacy in francophone West Africa. However, years of corruption and mismanagement had slowly transformed into political disaster for the country.

When Houphouët-Boigny died in December 1993 he was succeeded by Henri Konan Bédié after a brief power struggle with the prime minister, Alassane Ouattara. Bédié immediately began scheming to fix the approaching election, and promoted a divisive nationalistic concept he called "Ivoirité": only those people whose grandparents on both sides of their family had been born in Côte d'Ivoire could be considered citizens. This narrow definition became a legal reality that disenfranchised many of the country's citizens in the north—who were, conveniently enough, supporters of Ouattara, Bédié's main rival for the presidency.

Houphouët-Boigny had many faults as a leader, but at least he had taken care not to enflame ethnic resentments. One of his most enlightened policies concerned the country's independence day. Every year, the official celebration was held at a different Ivorian city—one year, it might take place in centrally located Bouaké; the next in Man, to the west; and the following year in northern Korhogo. People from all over Côte d'Ivoire would travel to the latest site for the independence-day festivities, and each year enjoy a patriotic holiday in an ethnic area different from their own. Clearly, Houphouët-Boigny had tried to strengthen a sense of nationhood while celebrating ethnic diversity.

If only his successor had understood this wisdom. By December 1999, ethnic and political resentments had simmered to the point of a military coup, which booted Bédié out of office and plunged the country into disorder. Opposition leader Laurent Gbagbo defeated the military-coup leader in an election the following year, but another coup attempt followed in 2001, and again in 2002. Gbagbo nominally held onto his office, but the last coup produced an official civil war that divided the country roughly in half. For readers interested in a fuller account of the national conflict, a good place to start is the anthropologist Mike McGovern's *Making War in Côte d'Ivoire*.

The Beng became one epicenter of the civil war thanks to the bad luck of geography: the Beng region straddles the boundary between the northern rebels and the government forces of the south. In 2002 a convoy of rebels invaded Bengland. Soon after, government soldiers surprised the rebel forces and attacked them. One village, Bongalo, was strafed and bombed. Nearby M'Bahiakro became a refugee camp, with internal exiles living in the town's schools and churches. Rebels then took control of the city of Bouaké, and many residents—including the Beng people living there—fled the city.

By the summer of 2004, the sorts of grisly and almost unreal headlines to which the West has become accustomed from other parts of postcolonial Africa had visited the Beng. The rebels forced farmers to hand over their crops, and they systematically raped Beng girls. Those villagers who could, escaped. At one point, the Beng villages were utterly empty: everyone had fled either to a neighboring region or hid in the deep forest. During the long period of occupation we, along with Bertin Kouadio, often waited for months for any word from Bengland.

Bertin had gained admission to the University of Illinois back in the spring of 1994, with a four-year scholarship. His BA in political science led him to an MA in African studies at Illinois, and then a doctoral program in international studies at Florida International University in Miami. In 2009, Bertin became the first Beng person to gain a doctorate, a story at once of triumph, dislocation, and loss, especially when one considers the title of his dissertation, "From

Stability to Insurgency: The Root and Proximate Causes of the September 2002 Civil War in Côte d'Ivoire." When Bertin returned to Côte d'Ivoire for a brief visit back in 2006, his parents sent word from Kosangbé warning him not to travel up-country. It was too dangerous—for him as well as for them. If the rebels didn't kill him when he entered the region, once he left they'd surely kill his parents, on the assumption that Bertin would have left money with them.

Meanwhile, Bertin has started a new life as a professor at Wilson College in Pennsylvania, where he is now the chair of the International Studies Program. His cultural and professional journey is worthy of a book, but it is not a book for us to write. We hope that one day Bertin will write it. And some day, when his home country begins to heal its deep wounds, Bertin plans to return and help the Beng recover. In the frustration of these intervening years, Alma has of necessity embarked on a new research project, with migrants from the West African island nation of Cape Verde, but we will not forget the Beng. As we did with *Parallel Worlds*, we will be donating royalties from *Braided Worlds* to the Beng, and we hope one day to return to Asagbé and Kosangbé, the villages where we have shared so much history and family.

UPDATE: APRIL 2012

The stories in any memoir do not end with the final pages; we offer some brief updates as of April 2012.

Amenan and her Ghanaian husband, Kofi, continue to work as farmers in Asagbé; their daughter Esi is grown and lives in Asagbé, as do Amenan's younger sister M'Akwé and Amenan's daughter Tahan and her now-grown son Meda. Nakoyan and her husband, Gaosu, remain in Asagbé as well, where Germain continues to serve as an elder. Yacouba still works as a farmer and healer in Kosangbé, while Mo'kissi has once again left the village. Ajengé works as a diviner in Prikro, a small town near Bengland. Dieudonné and his wife, Adèle, now live in Abidjan, and Augustin teaches French in an Ivorian high school. Nathaniel/N'zri Denju lives in California, where he works as a computer software engineer at Apple headquarters and is married to Emily Mell, a writer who spent her first five years living on a Navajo reservation in Arizona. Our second child, Hannah, now a teenager, has never been to Bengland, though she has accompanied us to Cape Verde and has traveled on her own to India.

Amenan's daughter Evelyne has passed on to the afterlife, as have Amenan's younger sister Ti, and her younger brother, Kofi Ba. Aba Kouassi, Jean, and Matatu have passed on to the afterlife, as have, in Kosangbé, San Yao, San Kofi,

Zang, Amlakro, and, most recently, Ché Kofi and Bertin's mother, Makola. Rest in peace.

As of this writing, Asagbé's mill is in a state of disrepair. Kosangbé's, water pump long broken, has recently been repaired, funded by initial royalties from *Braided Worlds*. Most of Kosangbé's blue chairs are gone, though a few remain in dilapidated shape. Kosangbé's tape deck and speakers were replaced years ago by a more modern system, and in these post–civil war days it still provides welcome weekend dance music that attracts youth from around Bengland.

.

A Brief Note about the Beng

With a population of about 12,000 in the West African nation of Côte d'Ivoire, the Beng are one of the smallest and least known of some sixty ethnic groups in a nation roughly the size of New Mexico. They inhabit an ecological border zone between the rain forest to the south and savanna to the north.

The majority of Beng people still live in relatively small, rural villages, where they practice a mixed economy of farming, hunting, and gathering. Both men and women work long hours in the fields much of the year, and children are trained in local farming techniques from the age of two or three years. In precolonial times, men hunted game regularly in the forest; however, the growth of a cash economy, with its more labor-intensive farming techniques based on monoculture, has reduced the time available for hunting. Women, men, and children continue to collect wild plants (especially berries and leaves), as well as trapping a variety of small forest creatures.

Beng families are usually large. In the villages, birth-control efforts are usually limited to a taboo on sex until a new baby can walk independently. Extended families typically consist of a husband and wife (or wives), all their unmarried daughters, all their sons, and their married sons' wives and children.

Until recently, virtually all Beng practiced their own religion, which requires people to offer prayers and sacrifices to sky/god (eci), ancestors, and a variety of bush and Earth spirits. Diviners use a variety of techniques to communicate with invisible spirits of the bush and of ancestors, and then interpret the spirits' communications to their concerned clients. Often, the divination indicates that a sacrifice to the Earth is necessary. In this case, the client then consults an Earth priest. These priests worship the Earth spirits according to the traditional six-day Beng calendar, offering prayers on behalf of people who seek protection against witchcraft, relief from afflictions deemed to have a spiritual cause, or atonement for past sins.

The Beng have probably maintained trade relations with neighboring groups for centuries (trading kola nuts, bush meat, and bark cloth for pottery, woven cloth, and machetes). Many Beng people now embrace Islam or Christianity—although they do not so much convert to these new religions as add them to their spiritual practices. In recent years, immigrants from the dry north have arrived to farm in Beng villages, thanks to the region's reputation for rich soils. To ensure that their children grow up able to speak with these various migrants and traders, Beng parents teach their sons and daughters to become multilingual from a very early age. Increasingly, they also send their children to public schools, where they learn French from first grade on.

Sadly, the Beng way of life has been threatened by Côte d'Ivoire's long political turmoil and civil war. The lingering effects of the country's most recent troubles remain to be documented.

Cast of Characters

Descriptions refer to the time of the events discussed in the book. Some of these names are pseudonyms to protect an individual's privacy; in other cases, we have used pseudonyms for clarity's sake because, as Philip has observed, "There were always so many Kofis."

Urbana, Illinois
>   Laura: trained midwife/anthropology student/medical student
>   Nathaniel: son of Alma and Philip

Abidjan, Côte d'Ivoire
>   Jean-Marie Adiaffi: Ivorian poet and playwright
>   Tanella Boni: Ivorian fiction writer
>   Jérôme Carlos: Ivorian novelist and poet
>   Bernard Dadié: Ivorian novelist and memoirist
>   Tiburce Koffi: Ivorian writer
>
>   Bertin Kouadio: Beng university student; oldest son of François and Makola in Kosangbé
>   Augustin: Beng university student
>   Ben Koffi Assida: former teacher of Bertin, turned businessman
>
>   Barbara Brown: development officer at the U.S. embassy
>
>   Pierre: middle-class Beng man
>   Stéphanie: Pierre's daughter

Village of Asagbé, Côte d'Ivoire
>   Akwé Amenan: village farmer; Alma's long-time friend and principal research collaborator
>   Kofi: Ghanaian husband of Amenan; native Fante speaker
>   Akissi Kro: mother of Amenan
>   Evelyne: adult daughter of Amenan
>   Kwamela: husband of Evelyne, working as a tailor in M'Bahiakro
>   Esi: thirteen-year-old daughter of Amenan
>   Baa: older brother of Amenan; village farmer and musician
>   Kofi Ba: adult younger brother of Amenan
>   Ti: adult younger sister of Amenan
>   Tahan: adult daughter of Amenan; mother of Meda

Meda: eight-year-old son of Tahan

Sassandra: six-month-old son of Tahan

M'Akwé: adult younger sister of Amenan; mother of Bapu and Chantal

Bapu: eleven-year-old son of M'Akwé

Chantal: two-and-a-half-year-old daughter of M'Akwé

Kokora (Aba) Kouassi: village Earth priest; maternal uncle of Amenan

Yao Kouassi: older brother of Kokora Kouassi

Bayo: red-haired adult daughter of Kokora Kouassi

Kouassi André: village farmer; our host in the village during our first month in the region in 1979; husband of Marie and Maat; father of Alise

Maat: second wife of Kouassi André

Alise: adult daughter of Kouassi André and his first wife, Marie

Thérèse: mother of Bandé, a sick newborn boy

Dieudonné: village farmer; husband of Adèle

Adèle: village farmer; wife of Dieudonné

Germain: village farmer; local secretary for the government party

N'zri Denju (Dangana): six-year-old reincarnation of a Beng ancestor

Matatu/Emmanuel: unstable young man; former barber of Asagbé

Yao: father of Matatu

Ajengé: young but powerful diviner who started to divine while a toddler

Sopi: elderly, childless woman

Nakoyan: adult daughter of Zang; wife of Gaosu; born in Kosangbé but living in Asagbé

Gaosu: Muslim farmer; husband of Nakoyan

Village of Kosangbé, Côte d'Ivoire

Yacouba: village farmer; close friend of Alma and Philip

Mo'kissi: runaway bride from 1980; friend of Alma

François: our Kosangbé village host in 1979–80; husband of Makola; father of Bertin

Makola: wife of François; mother of Bertin

San Kofi: village chief; younger brother of San Yao

San Yao: former village chief; older brother of San Kofi

Ché Kofi: village farmer; village chief's speaker

Zang: village farmer; father of Amlakro and Nakoyan

Amlakro: daughter of Zang; sister of Nakoyan; considered a "snake child"

Other Villages, Côte d'Ivoire

Gideon: immigrant Ghanaian carpenter

Kona Kofi Jean: petty trader in Bongalo; Alma's research assistant the first few months of our village stay in 1979 – 80

Ajei: immigrant Ghanaian healer living in Kaklagbé

Other Characters

Al Votaw: U.S. government official; friend of Alma and Philip

Esti Votaw: wife of Al Votaw; friend of Alma and Philip

Félix Houphouët-Boigny: president of Côte d'Ivoire, 1960 – 93

Henri Konan Bédié: president of Côte d'Ivoire, 1993 – 99

Laurent Gbagbo: president of Côte d'Ivoire, 2000 – 2011

Alassane Ouattara: former prime minister of Côte d'Ivoire; opposition political leader widely acknowledged to have won the November 2010 presidential election against Laurent Gbagbo; assumed the presidency in April 2011, after a violent, five-month electoral stalemate

Henry (Hank) Drewal: art historian specializing in West Africa

Tintin: hero of a series of books by the Belgian author Hergé

Glossary

For Beng words, we use spellings that most closely approximate how they would sound to an ordinary native English speaker; more technically accurate spellings using the standard International Phonetic Alphabet are found in Alma's Beng-English dictionary. Several dialects exist across Beng villages; in most cases, the spellings here refer to pronunciation common in the Forest dialect, especially in Kosangbé.

aba father, term of respect (Beng/Arabic)

àbibo diarrhea producing a foul-smelling gas (Beng)

agouti a rodent commonly hunted as meat in Côte d'Ivoire, also known as bush rat (French)

àh grîh grîh ey it's not a big deal, it's nothing serious (Beng)

a kunlia expression of sympathy or condolence (for an illness, death, or other misfortune) (Beng)

an'a let's go (Beng)

asé kpa nené wé how's everything? (lit., is everything cool here?) (Beng)

attieké couscous-like grain made from grated and slightly fermented manioc, eaten widely in southern Côte d'Ivoire (Ivorian French)

aung all-purpose female response (Beng)

auuuuuu exclamation of surprise, or full/complete understanding of a story or situation (Beng)

Bac university entrance exam (French)

Ba Feh Bey a rest day observed in the savanna region, in the traditional six-day Beng calendar (Beng)

bidon plastic jug (French)

blé kinlé asthma (lit., cut the sides) (Beng)

bouffer to unethically claim (or outright steal) funds from a government, individual, or business (lit., to eat) (Ivorian French slang)

bubu Muslim-style men's robe (Wolof, Ivorian French)

CFA franc currency used by eight (mostly French-speaking) nations in West Africa since 1945; formerly had a fixed exchange rate with the French franc, currently tied to the euro (French)

dangana silly, bizarre, or degenerate; can be an insult or a friendly tease (Beng) *eci* god; sky

fewa funeral performed for parents who have lost their first child (Beng)

gan klé lali formal speaker for a village chief, or for any individual or group
    engaging in a formal speaking situation (Beng)

gbri dirt; a disease of infants caused by contact with adults deemed
    symbolically dirty from certain sexual misdeeds (Beng)

ka ma dré great work; keep up the good work

ka nuwalé thank you (Beng)

kapok tree enormous tropical tree (*Ceiba pentandra*) ritually planted in
    every Beng village as the spiritual and social center of the village (English/
    Malay)

ka yi mi? do you want some water? (lit., [will] you drink water?) (Beng)

kutuku illegally home-brewed distilled alcohol (Beng)

les onzes insulting term for pedestrians judged too poor to afford to take a taxi
    or bus (lit., the elevens) (Ivorian French)

maa all-purpose male response (Beng)

maquis casual open-air bar/restaurant in a city or town (French)

na ka kwau mother[s], good afternoon (said to a woman or group of women
    of the age or generation of one's mother) (Beng)

ngo drewolo they're working (Beng)

ngo mi si paw? what's your name? (lit., what do they call you?) (Beng)

ngo séwé chalo they're reading (lit., they're looking at paper) (Beng)

n no n seyenlo I have a stomach-ache (Beng)

nongo older brother (Beng)

non, pas ici no, not here (French)

n'zri grandpa (lit., my grandfather) (Beng)

o geng kpang that's really good

pagne printed cloth, sold locally in one-meter lengths; long wrap-around skirt
    made from this cloth (French)

pen pú láná local plant used medicinally to treat dysentery (Beng)

piste dirt road or path (French)

propro zó láná local plant used medicinally to treat a fever (Beng)

sraka Beng sacrifice of an appealing food offered to village children (Beng/
    Arabic)

tété a bad omen (usually presaging a death) (Beng)

trelén local plant used medicinally to treat *àbibo* (Beng)

trobi trobi toothless (usually in reference to infants and the very elderly);
    slippery mouth (Beng)

wali popular board game played throughout Africa (commonly called *mancala*) (Beng)

wurugbé the Beng afterlife (lit., city of ancestors) (Beng)

yi glacé ice water (*yi* from Jula, "water"; *glacé* from French, "frozen")

yowlé gré stubborn personality (lit., strong eye) (Beng)

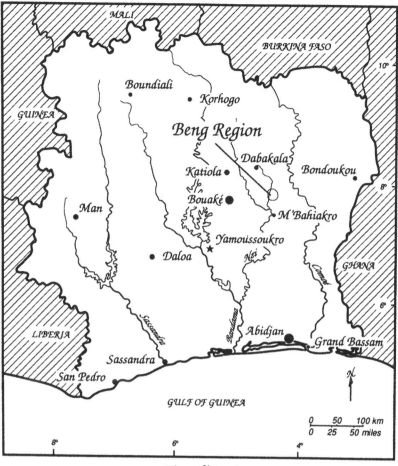

Côte d'Ivoire

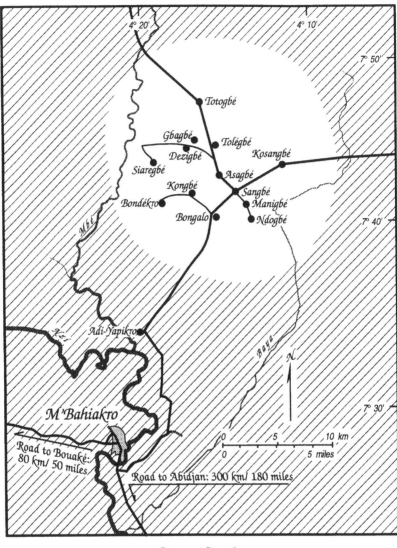

Beng Region

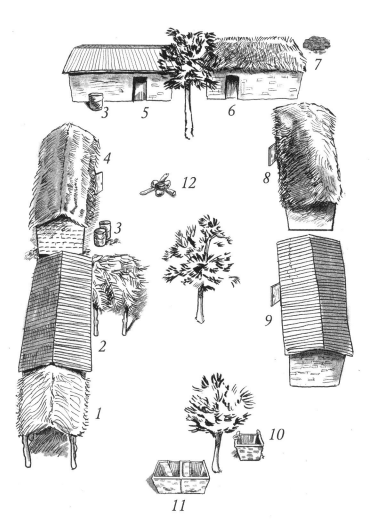

Amenan's Compound, 1993

1. Thatched gathering place
2. Sleeping quarters—Philip, Alma, and Nathaniel
3. Water barrels
4. Storage building
5. Amenan's family sleeping quarters
6. Granary

7. Old mud bricks
8. Food storage
9. Additional family sleeping quarters
10. Old bath house
11. Bath house and toilet stall
12. Cooking hearthstones

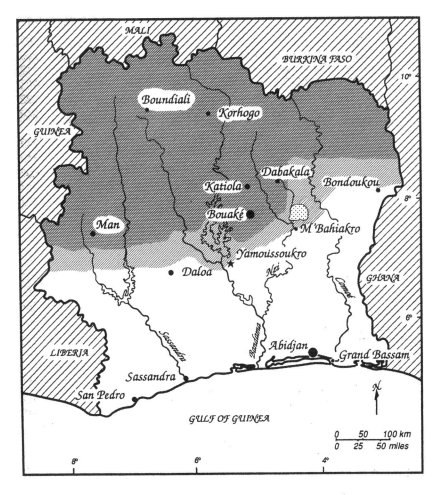

Côte d'Ivoire's Civil War and the Beng Region, ca. 2006

Northern Zone (Rebel-Controlled)

Disputed Zone

Beng Region

Southern Zone (Government-Controlled)

Acknowledgments

Any book long in the making inevitably accrues many debts. For inspiring conversations over the years about living in and writing about Africa and beyond, we are grateful to Sophia Balakian, Luís Batalha, Merle Bowen, Liora Bresler, Barbara Brown, Ed Bruner, Catarina Costa, JoAnn D'Alisera, Pamela Feldman-Savelsberg, Eric Gable, Robin Hemley, Michelle Johnson, Roy Kesey, Bertin Kouadio, Tim Landry, Lance Larkin, Harry Liebersohn, Michele Morano, Jennifer Nourse, Charlie Piot, Fernanda Pratas, Dorothée Schneider, Linda Seligmann, Mayumi Shimose-Poe, Paul Stoller, Nicole Tami, João Vasconcelos, Bjorn Westgard, Cindy Williams, Steve Wooten, Xu Xi, Paul Zeleza, and Rui Zink.

At the University of Chicago Press, David Brent has remained as patient and encouraging as an editor can be. Also, our thanks to Joann Hoy for careful copy editing, to Chuck Stout and B. W. Fore for the maps, and to Giulia Mazza for research assistance.

It goes without saying that our ongoing responsibility to the people of Bengland remains far outside the scope of these acknowledgments. We remain committed to devoting the proceeds from both *Parallel Worlds* and *Braided Worlds* to the Beng, all the while realizing the insufficiency of these efforts when compared with the gift of their observations and reflections offered to us over the years. To name just a few, we are more grateful than we can express to Amenan Véronique Akpoueh, Yacouba Kouadio Ba, Dieudonné Kwame Kouassi, Augustin Kouakou Yao, Bertin Kouakou Kouadio, Ajengé, and the late Kokora Kouassi—and to the many other Beng friends and neighbors who have hosted us and agreed to share their lives with us on different occasions.

For inspiring him to take seriously the moral responsibilities of a writer, Philip forever remains in debt to his former teacher, the late Grace Paley.

We first drafted this book commuting between several charming cafés and *pastelarias* in Lisbon, Portugal; their delicious teas, coffees, and pastries surely helped reawaken old memories.

Finally, our two children, Nathaniel and Hannah, didn't ask to be parented by a writer and an anthropologist, and we are grateful for their patience with their internationally gallivanting parents; we love and admire them both more than we can say.

Philip's position as the American Guest at the first Ivorian Writers Conference of 1990 was sponsored and funded by the American Cultural Center and the U.S. Department of State. For financial support of her research during summer 1993, Alma is grateful to the National Endowment for the Humanities; Wenner-Gren Foundation; and several units at the University of Illinois at Urbana-Champaign (including International Programs and Studies for a William and Flora Hewlett Faculty Award, and the Center for African Studies). For supporting the writing of this manuscript, we are both grateful for our two sabbatical leaves, and to our campus Research Board for our two Humanities Released

Time grants. We offer thanks for a different sort of help from Jesse Delia in his role as dean of the College of Liberal Arts at the university for supporting Bertin's studies at the University of Illinois.

We are grateful to several journal editors and book publishers for allowing us to reprint revised versions of short sections from the following previously published material:

Alma Gottlieb, "The Anthropologist as Mother: Reflections on Childbirth Observed and Childbirth Experienced," in *Anthropology Today* (1995), with a revised version in *The Afterlife Is Where We Come From: The Culture of Infancy in West Africa* (University of Chicago Press, 2004).

Alma Gottlieb and Philip Graham, "Mad to Be Modern," in *Being There: Learning to Live Cross-Culturally*, ed. Melvin Konner and Sarah Davis (Harvard University Press, 2011).

Alma Gottlieb and Philip Graham, "Our Village Needs Chairs," in *Bridges to Friendship: Narratives on Fieldwork and Friendship*, ed. Bruce Grindal and Frank Salamone (second, revised edition; Waveland Press, 2006).

Alma Gottlieb and Philip Graham, "Revising the Text, Revisioning the Field: Reciprocity over the Long Term," in *Anthropology and Humanism* (1999).

Alma Gottlieb, Philip Graham, and Nathaniel Gottlieb-Graham, "Infants, Ancestors and the Afterlife: Fieldwork's Family Values," in *Anthropology and Humanism* (1998).

Philip Graham, "Our Own House of Mbari," *Mid-American Review* (1991).

Philip Graham, "So Who Says Objects Are Inanimate?" and "Particle and Wave," in *McSweeney's Internet Tendency* (2006, 2008), and included in his collection, *The Moon, Come to Earth: Dispatches from Lisbon* (University of Chicago Press, 2009).

Index

Page numbers in italics refer to maps.

health: care given by AG and PG, 43, 45,
    82–83, 107–8; malnutrition, 82–83;
    PG's illness, 92–93, 97–98, 107; sick
    baby, 55–58, 68–69; tetanus, 56;
    yellow fever, 114. *See also* diviners and
    healers; mental illness
Hotel Ivoire, 18
Houphouët-Boigny, Félix, 11–12, 16, 23,
    107, 127, 131, 136–37
Hove, Chenjerai: *Bones*, 98

Igbo, 18–19
independence day, 137
infants. *See* children and babies
Infants de Mandela, Les (Carlos), 13
insects and spiders, 35, 36
International Phonetic Alphabet, 28, 69
Islam, 88, 111, 125, 141
Ivory Coast. *See* Côte d'Ivoire

Jean, 17, 50–51, 72, 75, 108–9, 138
jewelry for newborns, 52–54, 57

Kenya, 18
Koffi, Tiburce, 12, 13
Kofi (Amenan's husband): and the car,
    38; and carpentry work, 47, 48, 65;
    disappearance of, 39, 72, 104, 126;
    helps PG when sick, 97; relationship
    with Nathaniel, 31, 32, 34, 66, 112; as
    translator, 101; update on, 138
Kofi Ba (Amenan's brother), 47, 112, 121,
    138
Kokora Kouassi: dreams of, 46, 89–90,
    98, 102, 127; farewells to, 125; and lost
    sheep, 121; names Nathaniel, 41–42,
    46; and PG's father's funeral, 80–81,
    82, 85–86, 96; update of, 138
Kosangbé, 30, 58–62, 91, 117–20
Kouadio, 8, 110
Kouadio Pascal, 106
Kouakou, 53
kutuku (homemade brew), 85

Kwamela, 104, 125

Laing, Kojo, 99
Lamine, 30
lantern, setting up of, 33–34
Laura (childbirth coach), 4–9
Legos, 29, 72–73, 128
literature: choosing books in Abidjan,
    75; and politics, 12–13; reading to
    Nathaniel, 34–37, 39, 75, 91, 130. *See
    also names of individual authors*

Maat, 115–17
machete, 108, 109
madness. *See* mental illness
Magic Mountain, The (Mann), 107
Making War in Côte d'Ivoire (McGovern), 137
Makola, 14, 123–24, 139
M'Akwé, 32, 138
malnutrition, 82–83
Mama Day (Naylor), 26
Mami Wata, 127
Mandela, Nelson, 13
Mann, Thomas: *The Magic Mountain*, 107
maps: of Amenan's compound, 153; of
    Beng region, 152; of civil war, 154; of
    Côte d'Ivoire, 151
markets, 4, 22–24, 33, 37, 46, 71–72,
    74, 108
marriage: arranged, 59, 68, 91–92;
    dances to encourage, 91–92; disagree-
    ments between wives, 58, 96; and
    divorce/separation/rupture, 39, 59,
    68–69, 72, 87; and writing, 25
Matatu: AG's and PG's fear of, 110,
    111–12, 114, 118; behavior of, 62–65,
    73–74, 81–82, 93–94, 109–10, 111–12;
    causes of mental illness, 64–65, 101–2,
    122, 132; first encounter with, 52; tied
    up, 81–82, 112; treatment for mental
    illness, 88–89, 100, 101–2, 109, 122;
    update of, 138
M'Bahiakro, 38, 39, 56–58, 137